Preparing
Tomorrow's
Missionaries
Today

Preparing
Tomorrow's
Missionaries
Today

Teaching Skills for Disciples of Christ

Robert Y. Cornilles

With Dr. Taylor Halverson

ISBN 978-1-951341-09-1
Published by Line of Sight Publishing.
Cover image by David Becker on Unsplash
Cover design © 2020 by Megan Lagerberg
Typeset by Deborah Spencer
Copyedited by Kathryn Jenkins

Dedication

To my late grandfather, Thomas Young Emmett, a beloved leader and persuasive communicator whose gift for teaching is undoubtedly hastening the gathering on the other side.

Contents

Acknowledgments

Truthfully, I'm a little self-conscious to state that I've written a book about missionary work.

No, I'm not ashamed of the topic or my offering. But the sacred work of gathering Israel through missionary efforts of the Church of Jesus Christ of Latter-day Saints is and always has been under the stewardship of the Quorum of the Twelve Apostles. I, on the other hand, am simply a lay member giving a small offering to the world-wide effort.

I'm also not the type of person who, without fail, talks to strangers on airplanes about my beliefs or tells people in the grocery line why I'm happy. My nature has been to try and be what President Gordon B. Hinckley described as one of the members whose "lives . . . become the most meaningful expression of our faith" ("The Symbol of Our Faith," *Ensign*, April 2005). (*Try* is the key word!) I am grateful, though, that the deeper my conversion, the more comfortable I am sharing, explaining, and testifying of those things that have made my life richer and full of meaning.

This project began several years ago, starting with the insistence of Jeff Brownlow, formerly a bold missionary serving in the Oregon Portland Mission where I used to live. Elder Brownlow arranged a meeting with me and his mission president, Dr. Van C. Gessel. After some discussion, President Gessel's invitation to conduct skills-based training to advance the use of *Preach My Gospel* in the mission sent me down this path. His successor, Elder Timothy J. Dyches, was also receptive to the work I had done within the mission. I thank them for their trust and confidence.

And though all the missionaries back then have long been sent home to obtain their education, start families and careers, and presumably do all kinds of good in the world, I owe much to their helpful feedback, which led us to record those trainings. Eventually, the recordings turned into a transcript, and that transcript became this book.

The person to whom I am most indebted for this content coming together is Tom Peterson, a former business associate who has remained a close and reliable friend. When he learned back then of the opportunity to turn my professional content into a missionary-facing training workshop, he not only took upon himself some of my work duties to free me up for the purpose, he also served as an indispensable advisor, confidante, sounding board, and early editor. Even today, as a professor at Brigham Young University's Marriott School of Business, Tom continues to be a loyal advocate of my professional work and the content I teach to MBA students as an adjunct professor at BYU.

Special thanks goes to Dr. Taylor Halverson, for without his insistence that I wipe the dust off this material and get it into print, it probably would not be a source of information today. Yes, he's an accomplished doctrinal writer, but he's more importantly my wise friend. His championing of this material and insistence that there is value in it motivated me to dive into a project I had longed to tackle but wasn't quite sure was worth the effort.

I thank Kathryn Jenkins for her friendship, support, and excellent ability to compile my thoughts and make them easier for those not in my head to understand.

I am grateful to all the full-time and ward missionaries I have ever met, worked with, taught with, learned from, and observed whose efforts and sacrifice convince me that of all of God's priorities, He is invested in nothing more important than bringing souls to Jesus Christ. (It's trite and has been said before, but if The Church of Jesus

Christ of Latter-day Saints wasn't true, we who have been allowed to serve missions and wear the name tag bearing His name would have ruined it a long time ago.) I am just one of millions who have or do engage in missionary work, so I am confident this book is a subconscious compilation of many people's learnings and wisdom from which I have benefited.

To Allison, my precious wife and companion, I express my deepest appreciation. She is patient, trusting, and has permitted me the time and space needed to dedicate my energies to a subject she knows means so very much to me.

Finally, I thank my Heavenly Father for allowing me the privilege to experience the making of this book. Any truths herein are not mine but are His. If there is something useful or helpful to the reader, it is due to His graciousness. I have just been the collator of what He has unveiled to many others and me. God declares and teaches these principles and practices better than anyone, but I thank Him for granting me the privilege to ponder, pray, and produce something that asserts my abiding testimony of Him.

Robert Y. Cornilles

Preface

"[The] gathering is the most important thing taking place on earth today. Every one of our Heavenly Father's children, on both sides of the veil, deserves to hear the message of the restored gospel of Jesus Christ."

President Russell M. Nelson, "Hope of Israel"
Worldwide Youth Devotional, June 3, 2018

WELCOME TO YOUR MISSION!

Those words should sound familiar.

Why? Because whether you've received a formal mission call and assignment from the prophet of the Lord or are anticipating one in the future, you are already on a mission. It began the day you were born! And you know what? It doesn't end the day you're formally released or the day you speak in sacrament meeting when you get back.

While addressing Aaronic Priesthood holders, Elder David A. Bednar said, "Each of you is a missionary now. All around you, every day, are friends and neighbors 'who are only kept from the truth because they know not where to find it' (Doctrine and Covenants 123:12). You need not and should not wait for your official call to become anxiously engaged in missionary work" ("Called to the Work," *Ensign*, May 2017).

So, no matter your circumstances, the Apostle Paul, one of the greatest missionaries to ever live, wanted all who assist in the Lord's work to see themselves as:

1

"Ambassadors for Christ" (2 Corinthians 5:20)
"Workers together with him" (2 Corinthians 6:1)
"Ministers of God" (2 Corinthians 6:4)
"A teacher of the Gentiles" (1 Timothy 2:7)
"A good soldier of Jesus Christ" (2 Timothy 2:3)

Whenever you decide to acknowledge that Paul was describing *you*, the principles, Christlike attributes, behaviors, stories, scenarios, and skills discussed in this book will begin to penetrate your mind and heart. And you'll realize that, like the sons of Alma, you are called to preach "after the holy order of God" (Alma 43:2).

No pressure.

So, as I said, welcome to your mission!

As you read the pages that follow, we will trace the remarkable journey of spreading the beauty and truth of the Lord's message as devoted participants in the gathering of God's children.

Let me share how this book came about.

Several years ago, two outstanding full-time missionaries stopped by my business on their preparation day. They wanted to visit about a referral. They arrived just as I was finishing up some skills-based training for a diverse group of clients who had come for that purpose. I invited the missionaries to observe from the back of the room as I was wrapping up the session.

As they would later report to their mission president, they watched me teach, and a funny thing happened. These two missionaries heard me train a group of professionals in ways consistent with what's recommended in *Preach My Gospel,* a recently published resource I had admittedly not yet read. Soon their mission president was visiting with me in my office. In that discussion, he concluded that my professional approach to teaching—borne undoubtedly from my experiences as a missionary, Church member, husband, father, neighbor, citizen, and businessperson—was aligned with and complemented the counsel in

Preach My Gospel and would help any missionary. This book is a result of others' prodding to share it with you.

***

Before I go any further, I need to let you know that this material is not an official publication of The Church of Jesus Christ of Latter-day Saints. I do not represent the Church or its leaders. I wasn't called or assigned to write this book. And though I had encouragement and assistance from key individuals named in the acknowledgments to complete this book, I'm completely responsible for any opinions or mistakes you may find. I *do* hope you will discover something in it to help in your missionary efforts. Please use it within the direction your authorized leaders have given, and never let it distract you from your daily study of the scriptures and of *Preach My Gospel.*

Speaking of *Preach My Gospel,* you might already know this: it caused a radical change in the way we do missionary work in the Church. A few years after the manual was first published in 2004, Elder Richard G. Scott said in general conference that the manual had "greatly improved sharing the gospel worldwide" ("Now Is the Time to Serve a Mission!" *Ensign,* May 2006). If you'd like to get an idea of how huge those improvements are, just talk to your parents or anyone else who served a mission back in the day. (Ask about those discussions they had to memorize. Together you will appreciate more the Savior's teachings that "old things are done away, and all things have become new" (3 Nephi 12:47).)

As you study that inspired manual and as you consider the words in this book, there's one thing you should never forget: none of it—not one bit—will succeed on its own, even with your talents and capabilities and good intentions thrown into the mix. You can be the best and the brightest and the most prepared missionary with access to the most amazing resources on earth, but none of it matters without one important thing.

The Spirit.

As President Ezra Taft Benson said, "The Spirit is the most important single element in this work. With the Spirit magnifying your call, you can do miracles for the Lord in the mission field. Without the Spirit, you will never succeed, regardless of your talent and ability" (*Preach My Gospel: A Guide to Missionary Service* [Salt Lake City: The Church of Jesus Christ of Latter-day Saints, 2019], 178).

Never forget that. Nothing in this book, nothing in *Preach My Gospel*, not even anything in the scriptures will contribute to your success as a missionary if it is not accompanied by the Spirit, who is the ultimate Teacher and Converter. Without the Spirit, your lessons and testimonies will ring hollow.

More than anything else you can do, then—more than getting all the right clothes, more than applying for your passport, more than passing your physical, more than finding a great pair of shoes and collecting the best ties on the planet, more than memorizing every scripture under the sun—is your commitment to living so you qualify for the constant companionship of the Holy Ghost. *That* is what will make you a powerful missionary who will bless the lives of those you teach.

Listen again to the Apostle Paul: "And my speech and my preaching was not with enticing words of man's wisdom, but in the demonstration of the Spirit and of power: That your faith should not stand in the wisdom of men, but in the power of God" (1 Corinthians 2:4–5).

This work, then, is my contribution to all missionaries who seek truth—wherever it may be found—in how to best *teach* truth. I hope this might be accepted with gladness, for "the righteous love the truth" (2 Nephi 9:40). Consider it more "line upon line, precept upon precept," given through the power of that same Holy Ghost that you will need to preach His gospel (see 2 Nephi 28:26–31). Just as we are taught the pattern to know the truth in all things (Moroni 10:4–6), I invite you to read this prayerfully, asking God to grant you the Holy Ghost so that you can know how this work may help—and never hinder—your holy calling.

SECTION I

Principles and Practices

"I teach them correct principles, and they govern themselves."

Joseph Smith,
as quoted by John Taylor in "Millennial Star"
15 November 1851, p. 339

**"A principle is an enduring truth, a law, a rule you
can adopt to guide you in making decisions."**

President Boyd K. Packer,
"The Word of Wisdom: The Principle and the Promises," *Ensign*, May 1996

The world would describe the grandfather to whom I have dedicated this book as a self-made man. With no formal education beyond
high school, he inherited the industriousness of his great-grandfather
Brigham Young, and supported his mother and two older sisters after
the death of his father. Though unable to serve a full-time mission due
to the unforeseen responsibilities at home, through grit, grind, and
faithfulness my grandfather developed the characteristics all great
missionaries must possess.

Thus resigned that he would serve the Lord at home instead of
abroad, 26-year old Thomas Young Emmett gathered one Sunday
morning with a group of Saints when, as was typical in those days,
President David O. McKay of the First Presidency called his name

and asked him to stand. He announced that Tom was to be called as a bishop, instructing him to move his family and establish a new ward—including the funding and construction of a chapel.

So began a lifetime of discipleship for Tom with its many challenges and blessings, both public and private. As he would often say, "I received my education through the School of LDS."

Like any great learner, my grandfather took his experiences and endeavored to teach them to others—whether in Church settings, home, business, or community. Up until his death just a few months shy of his 102nd birthday in 2013, he never stopped teaching. I benefited from Tom's own lectures on faith.

Two ideas stand out amongst all his lessons:

1. "More than remembering what you say, people will remember how you made them *feel*."
2. "Putting aside all the policies and programs of the Church, remember that it's the *principle* that matters."

In Chapters 1–4 of this book, we will explore how a disciple of Christ can help others *feel* the love and concern of their Savior, the guidance of His Spirit, and the righteous intent of the servants who carry His message. We will also identify helpful *principles and practices* that should guide missionaries when they teach, and which most certainly influence the choices and decisions of investigators.

Chapter One

"Proclaim His Gospel"

Teaching to Match Our Message

**"Behold, I am a disciple of Jesus Christ, the Son of God.
I have been called of him to declare his word among his
people, that they might have everlasting life."**

Mormon, 3 Nephi 5:13

As a member or full-time missionary for The Church of Jesus Christ of Latter-day Saints, you possess two things no one else does.

First, you have the greatest message on earth—the message of the restored gospel of Jesus Christ, often called the "good news."

"Wherefore, how great the importance to make these things known unto the inhabitants of the earth" (2 Nephi 2:8).

Second, you're called, authorized, and hold the power to deliver that good news to the world. You are sustained by the Holy Ghost to testify of its truthfulness.

With those two gifts, you're set. Right? Maybe. Consider this: how sad to have the greatest message on earth and the authority to deliver it, accompanied by the Spirit, but *not be able to deliver it to the best of your ability*. It's like having the most beautiful cake ever created and hungry friends and family ready to eat it, then realizing you don't have any plates and forks! You need to be able to teach the most wonderful message on earth in a way that it will be received and accepted by those waiting and wanting to hear it.

Face it. The gospel and the Spirit will go on without you and me. But there's one valuable thing full-time missionaries can bring to this worldwide effort. Any idea what that might be? Of course, a positive, prayerful, and faithful attitude is critical. But the one thing you probably haven't spent as much time thinking about before your missionary service begins is *effective teaching skills.* Teaching methods to match your message. Pair that up with the Spirit, and you'll be unstoppable in persuading people to listen and come to Jesus Christ, their Savior and Redeemer.

There are many in the Church who want to be good member missionaries. Most of them have tremendous goodwill. And the Church has a multitude of missionaries dedicated to spreading the good news. After all, who doesn't want to persuade others to take more than a passing interest in what we know will bring eternal happiness?

What happens, then? Why do so many of those efforts fall short? Because in many cases, members and missionaries alike know *what* to say but don't exactly know *how* to say it.

Don't get too stressed about that. When you desire to share what is in your heart, according to Elder Dieter F. Uchtdorf, "Talking with others about your faith will become normal and natural. In fact, the gospel will be such an essential, precious part of your lives that it would feel unnatural *not* to talk about it with others" ("Missionary Work: Sharing What is in Your Heart," *Ensign,* Nov. 2019).

Of course, this effort needs to be supported with study and experience living the teachings of the gospel. Then it is fine-tuned by acquiring powerful teaching skills.

Early in his mission, a young Gordon B. Hinckley was discouraged. He wrote a letter to his father complaining that the work was hard and that the people weren't receptive. He pretty much wanted to give up. To come home. The letter he got back from his father contained now well-known advice that every missionary should remember: "Forget yourself and go to work" ("Sweet Is the Work: President Gordon B. Hinckley, 15th President of the Church," *New Era,* May 1995).

Getting to work will give you experience. But training can accelerate your learning as you gain experience. In other words, if trained properly, you can avoid many common mistakes missionaries inadvertently make, and you will more quickly experience real success.

So fasten your seatbelt as we speed up your experience through the training and suggestions you'll find in this book. But don't think you're going to be reading about untested theories or ideas. Gratefully, many have already reported vast improvement in their skills and abilities talking with friends, teaching, and interacting with members through the ideas presented here. They have found this only enhances their use of *Preach My Gospel*, the most inspired tool ever produced for the work of missionaries.

Most of what follows focuses on the principles in Chapter Ten of *Preach My Gospel*, which is appropriately titled, "How Can I Improve My Teaching Skills?" I'll point out specific scriptures and teachings from General Authorities, many of which are found in that chapter. I'll also share conversations I've had with missionaries and some awesome experiences I and others have had using these concepts. Always keep in mind, though, that my approach and ideas aren't the "only way" to do things; I'm offering them here for your consideration and application.

The first words in *Preach My Gospel* are to you from the First Presidency: "Dear Fellow Missionary" (*Preach My Gospel*, v). Isn't it amazing to realize that you and the First Presidency share the privilege of being missionaries?

Beyond being cool, those simple words convey an important principle: You are a witness of Christ. You know that an Apostle's calling requires him to be a "special witness." Always remember that whether you're an Apostle, a full-time missionary, or a lay member, you are also a witness and messenger for the Savior.

In that opening message, the First Presidency assures you, "*Preach My Gospel* is intended to help you be a better-prepared, more spiritually mature missionary and a more *persuasive teacher*" (*Preach My Gospel*, v; emphasis added). Keep that in mind as we walk together through the steps to become a better prepared teacher.

Teaching is central to everything you do as a missionary. "You develop Christlike attributes, study the missionary lessons, improve your ability to speak in your mission language, and rely on the Spirit in order to teach with convincing power" (*Preach My Gospel*, 177).

Ready to get started? Great! As President Hinckley's father counseled, let's get to work!

Follow Impressions

I join with so many others in praying that, as you undertake this important work, you'll receive information, insights, and impressions—that they will come into your mind and heart as you study and teach.

When that happens, do as President Thomas S. Monson repeatedly taught: If you feel an impression, *follow it*. Don't put it off. Put it into action. As you commit to become a better teacher and to follow the impressions you receive, you will be rewarded—and so will the people you teach.

Whenever these impressions occur, *write them down*. They are messages given to you by the one companion you're entitled to always have—the Spirit. And you will want to remember them.

My grandfather always taught me that "perspiration precedes inspiration." The Spirit works not only when you're out *doing* missionary work, but it also works when you're diligently *preparing* for the work. Consider that carefully. I don't think it's an accident that the Brethren provided space for taking notes on every page of *Preach My Gospel*.

As you take notes, you might find the Spirit whispering to you that the skill or technique you're studying is one you can use with someone you're already teaching—or even someone you haven't yet contacted. Maybe the Spirit will show you how something you're reading will help you and your companion become more effective teaching partners. Perhaps a principle you read here will help you in your district, as a member of your zone, or even in the emails you send or phone calls you make to home.

Learn the Language of the Lord

Depending on where you are called to serve, you might need to learn a foreign language. On the day of Pentecost in the New Testament, thousands of Jews from many nations gathered in Jerusalem and rejoiced, "We do hear them speak in our tongues the wonderful works of God" (Acts 2:11). How could they rejoice if they couldn't understand what was being said? Or, as Paul says in Romans, "So then faith cometh by hearing, and hearing by the word of God" (Romans 10:17). And Alma taught his son Corianton, "Ye are called of God to preach the word unto this people . . . declare the word with truth and soberness, that thou mayest bring souls unto repentance, that the great plan of mercy may have claim upon them" (Alma 42:31). Corianton couldn't do that without speaking in the language of the listener. And neither can you or the hundreds of thousands of missionaries before you. Thus, great care is taken to prepare missionaries to speak in more than sixty languages.

But no matter where you are called to serve, you need to commit to speak in the language of the Lord.

Speaking in someone's native tongue and speaking in the language of the Lord are two very different things. Let me explain.

When you get that big envelope in the mail or that eagerly anticipated email inviting you to accept the call to become a missionary, you might be wishing to be sent on a foreign-speaking mission. Lots of missionaries—as well as their family and friends—hope for that for a variety of reasons, I presume. Once you're fully engaged in the work, though, you'll quickly realize that, as President J. Reuben Clark once said, "In the service of the Lord, it is not where you serve, but how" (Conference Report, April 1951, 151).

I was called to serve and was assigned to a mission in Japan. I was excited to learn a new language. But I soon thought my friends assigned to English-speaking missions had an advantage over me. First, they got to learn all the hymns in English. (I hear you never realize what a blessing that is until you try to warble "The Spirit of God" in Finnish.)

That's not all. While I was trying to learn and master a foreign language, I thought about my English-speaking missionary friends who could spend that study time diving deep into the scriptures. I figured that must have made their teaching richer than mine and their understanding of the doctrines more profound than mine. (I've since learned that may or may not be the case.)

But listen up: *every missionary needs to learn a new language.* Even if you're assigned to labor in your native tongue, that new way of speaking you must master is the language of the Lord as found in the scriptures.

President Ezra Taft Benson explained, "The words and the way they are used in the Book of Mormon by the Lord . . . should be used by us in teaching gospel principles" ("The Book of Mormon and the Doctrine and Covenants," *Ensign*, May 1987, 84; *Preach My Gospel*, 182). Learning the "language of the Lord" as found in the Book of Mormon and using it in all your teaching is certainly as challenging as learning any "foreign language."

No matter where you labor, strive to speak and teach as the Savior did—and as the missionaries and prophets in the Book of Mormon taught. That's not impossible. But it takes time and practice. And it absolutely takes study and the development of skills. "We study," said Elder D. Todd Christofferson, "so that we may better teach" ("The Priesthood Quorum," *Ensign*, Nov. 1998).

Recognize and Develop Gifts

We learn in the Doctrine and Covenants that all of us have different gifts (see D&C 46:11–29). For some, it's a gift of faith. Others may have the gift of administration. Some may have the power of discernment—or other gifts of the Spirit. Counsel with the Lord and learn which gifts you have "according to the grace that is given to us" (Romans 12:6). Then develop them so you can serve a more rewarding mission.

If one of the gifts you'd really like to obtain as a missionary is teaching, or communicating, or developing love and sympathy for others, the material on the pages that follow can serve as your guide to acquire and develop those heavenly gifts.

Three Things to Know

Since you have accepted or are just about to willingly accept the call to serve a full-time mission, I'm assuming you have a good work ethic and enthusiasm for teaching the gospel. Most missionaries do. You'll find, though, that the willingness to work hard and a good attitude aren't always enough for consistent, effective missionary work. They help, of course, but only when combined with three other things.

1. **You must know the Spirit and seek to be His companion.**
2. **You must know the principles of the gospel you're teaching.**
3. **You must know how to communicate what you learn from the Spirit, the scriptures, and prophets.**

Seek the Spirit

My former mission president, Toshiro Yoshizawa, didn't speak much English. But the one sentence he did know punctuated every one of his talks: "You must have the Spirit!"

If you find yourself at times falling short as a missionary, it might be because the Spirit is only your *sometimes* companion, not your constant companion. That could be due to something you're doing—or not doing—that is disqualifying you from working in tandem with Him.

Note what the Lord indicates must not only come first, but must remain with His missionaries in order for them to successfully do His work: "But ye shall receive power, after that the Holy Ghost is come upon you; and ye shall be witnesses unto me . . . unto the uttermost part of the earth" (Acts 1:8).

That's not to say that when you are accompanied by the Holy Ghost that you will be shielded from all problems. Even Spirit-filled missionaries have challenges—and should in a world that revolves around agency. You'll remember accounts of missionaries and prophets in the Bible and the Book of Mormon who were faithful representatives of the Savior, yet still faced immense challenges. Examples of those read like a "Who's Who" of amazing missionaries: Esther, Ruth, Peter, Paul, Stephen, Priscilla, Lehi, Nephi, Jacob, Abinadi, Alma, Alma the Younger, Aaron, Ammon, Amulek, Samuel the Lamanite, Nephi (son of Helaman), Mormon, and Moroni, just to name a few.

Fact is, in the scriptures you'd be hard-pressed to find even one missionary who *didn't* have extraordinary trials. All were rejected at one time or another. Some were driven out of cities. Some had to give up their friends, family, and livelihood. And some even lost their lives for the sake of the gospel. If even these great women and men of scripture had obstacles to overcome, why should today's missionaries be exempt?

That being said, "For as many as are led by the Spirit of God, they are the sons [and daughters] of God" (Romans 8:14). The Spirit will help you as the sons and daughters of God in all your labors and will instruct and inspire you during challenging times. Simply put, you can't do it without Him.

Learn the Doctrine

"Seek not to declare my word, but first seek to obtain my word, and then shall your tongue be loosed; then, if you desire, you shall have my Spirit and my word, yea, the power of God unto the convincing of men" (D&C 11:21).

Another reason you may not experience success is that you lack knowledge of the gospel and its doctrines. An indispensable part of your daily study must be the scriptures, teachings of the living prophets, and *Preach My Gospel*. Consistent effort at learning and living the gospel will expand your knowledge and testimony of the good news of Christ.

It only stands to reason that you can't teach what you don't know. And you can't *effectively* teach what you don't live. Ignoring your individual compass—your personal Liahona—will, as Alma taught his son

Helaman, cause unnecessary failure. "They [our fathers] were slothful, and forgot to exercise their faith and diligence and then those marvelous works ceased, and they did not progress in their journey" (Alma 37:41).

Develop the Necessary Skills

The third factor that may prevent you from your highest potential as a missionary is a lack of the skills needed to communicate with God's diverse children. If you desire to teach with power, *Preach My Gospel* is a divine resource given you to develop valuable skills for effectively carrying your message.

During the summer after my freshman year at Brigham Young University and before I reported to the Missionary Training Center, I got a job as a bill collector in one of the roughest sections of my hometown of Portland, Oregon. Put yourself in my place and imagine how fun it would be to collect bills in a very poor area of a major city.

Day after day I knocked on doors, reminding people that their bills were delinquent. I was instructed to warn them that if they didn't pay me right there on the spot, their service would be canceled. Whenever I tell my Portland friends about my summer job that year, they laugh and look at me like *What were you thinking?!* I was too inexperienced and naïve to know how risky the job was.

Why do I share this story? Three reasons.

First, there's no better way to prepare for the rigors of a mission than to do hard things before you're called. I'm not talking crazy things like living alone in the wild for a month or rappelling down skyscrapers or putting your head in a nest of scorpions. I'm talking about meaningful experiences that will stretch your abilities and, yes, even your faith. Volunteer to go visit that less-active member in the ward or organize a clean-up of the yard for the man who's down with an illness. In other words, prepare for a full-time mission by being a fully engaged minister.

Second, the experience I gained as a bill collector helped me significantly as a full-time missionary whose primary means for finding investigators was to knock on doors. The experience of doing so in Portland and asking people to pay me their past-due bills was great preparation for what I eventually did in the name of the Lord. I was better able to brush off the rejection of knocks going unanswered or doors slamming in my face. (Yes, it happens.) I don't think it will ever get as bad for you as it did for Alma: "Now when the people withstood all his words, and reviled him, and spit upon him, and caused that he should be cast out of their city, he departed thence" [Alma 8:13]), but as a set-apart missionary, "when ye do well, and suffer for it, ye take it patiently, this is acceptable with God" (1 Peter 2:20).

The third reason for sharing this story is that the skills you develop as a missionary will benefit you (and those you love) throughout your entire life—including all other assignments you receive as a member of the Church. Those skills don't come without faithful effort.

***

I once asked a group of missionaries what skills served them best on their mission. Their responses could be a checklist:

- The ability to relate to others.
- The ability to listen.
- The ability to memorize (names, a new language, the mission motto, scriptures).
- Boldness—courage in proclaiming the gospel.
- A spirit of optimism—always being hopeful.
- The ability to discern—a power granted to missionaries.
- The ability to plan—recognizing that spiritual experiences for investigators come from your planning and execution of lessons well taught.
- The development of Christlike attributes, including how to get along with a companion; learning patience, forgiveness, and obedience.

Let's not forget: as a missionary, there's one skill or gift you are set apart to master. It's the skill of teaching. There is "no greater call." You may already have that skill, or you might be struggling with it. It's a skill you will need throughout your life—in any calling you accept within the Church, as a parent, and as a contributing member of your community. But you'll probably never have a greater opportunity to hone the skill of effective teaching than during the time consecrated for nothing but missionary work. So, use this time to become more proficient at excellent, Spirit-guided teaching.

Learn the PIC-ture Skills

Consider again the First Presidency's introduction to *Preach My Gospel*. It makes clear that the purpose of the manual is to help you become "a more persuasive teacher" (*Preach My Gospel*, v). "PIC-ture" this, then:

Persuade
Influence
Convince

Combined, there are nearly a hundred scriptural references to the words *persuade, influence,* and *convince.* The Lord has always needed His missionaries to master each in order to combat the adversary's expertise at the same.

Before we explore this further, you must be clear on one common misconception:

"May I remind you that God does not need you to 'sell' the restored gospel or the Church of Jesus Christ" (Dieter F. Uchtdorf, "Your Great Adventure," *Ensign*, Nov. 2019).

"When we invite you to attend church with us or to learn with the full-time missionaries, we are not trying to sell you a product" (David A. Bednar, "Come and See," *Ensign*, May 2014).

How could we ever approach the notion that the glorious gospel of Jesus Christ is like a product someone must purchase? The only thing that's been purchased is the sins of those we meet—and that was done by a Savior who simply wants us to find, teach, and serve those He has redeemed.

It's instructive to examine the Master Persuader-Influencer-Convincer. Observe how He uses these teaching tools for the betterment of those He teaches:

"And now come, sayeth the Lord, by the Spirit, unto the elders of his Church, and let us reason together, that you may understand; Let us reason even as a man reasoneth one with another face to face" (D&C 50:10–11).

Think about that: How do most missionaries talk to investigators? Just as the Lord suggests: face to face. When you're teaching, you're *reasoning* with people. You're not trying to get them to do something they don't want to do. You're "not walking in craftiness, nor handling the word of God deceitfully" (2 Corinthians 4:2). No. You're trying to help them remember something they once agreed with and agreed to—a reality they once knew. And by using sound reasoning, your investigator's spirit is more likely to recall the truthfulness of the gospel.

The next verse goes further: "Now, when a man reasoneth he is understood of man, because he reasoneth as a man; even so will I, the Lord, reason with you that you may understand" (D&C 50:12). The Lord is setting a teaching example for us. He wants you to reason with people in a way they will understand. By nature, reasoning leads to understanding.

During his mission, Paul adopted this wonderful teaching trait: "And Paul, *as his manner was*, went in unto them, and three sabbath days *reasoned* with them out of the scriptures" (Acts 17:2; emphasis added).

Reasoning, though, doesn't necessarily lead to agreement. Though things may be logical and clear to you, some people may choose to disagree. After all, most of those who lived in the days of Paul heard what we would consider wonderful missionary teaching, and still walked away, unconvinced (see Acts 28:22–24). But if what you teach is reasonable and is done in a sensible way, your investigator might just think, *That sounds pretty reasonable. Hmmm, I'll think about what they said.*

What happens then? The Book of Mormon describes it as a "seed." What you taught might begin to take root and grow in that person. (You can read about that in Alma 32:28–43.) And given time, that person might open his or her heart, allowing the Holy Ghost to testify that what you taught was true. Reasoning turns into influencing, which turns into agreement, which turns into conversion.

But let's step back and take a modern-day look at the big PICture (persuade, influence, convince). I used to think that *convincing*, for instance, was sort of negative—almost like besting your opponent to win an argument. It depends, however, on the purpose of your convincing. Trying to "convince people against their will" is sometimes dangerous because, as the old saying goes, "they are of the same opinion still" (Dale Carnegie, *How to Win Friends and Influence People* [New York: Simon & Schuster Inc., 1981]. In other words, their minds really aren't changed. Having not been truly persuaded, they're just worn down by your insistence. Thinking you've convinced others, but without the Spirit, can also do a lot of damage to our work of gathering Israel.

But convincing people *with* the Spirit leads to magnificent blessings. Examine the case of the early Church in the Book of Mormon. How did Alma, a one-time wicked priest of King Noah, come to know of his Savior and the gospel? He heard it convincingly preached. Listen, then, to his son recount how the founding of the early Church began:

"Did not my father Alma believe in the words which were delivered by the mouth of Abinadi? . . . Did he not speak the words of God, and my father Alma believe him? And according to his faith there was a mighty change wrought in his heart. And behold, he preached the word unto your fathers, and a mighty change was also wrought in their hearts" (Alma 5:11–13). By persuading others with Spirit-fed words, life-improving decisions and life-saving changes can occur. Conceivably, without Abinadi's power to convince and persuade, the Book of Mormon story would have ended there. But because of Abinadi's teaching abilities, the Church was established by his unknown investigator, Alma.

So, with so much responsibility at the feet of those whose feet "bringeth good tidings" (Isaiah 52:7; Mosiah 12:21; 3 Nephi 20:40), how exactly can you learn the PIC-ture skills? After all, in your youth you probably didn't have a ward activity where the leader announced, "This week we're going to prepare for missions by teaching you how to be more convincing." Yeah, probably not.

As we did with Paul, let's look at another great missionary's example:

In 1 Nephi 3:21, Nephi explains: "And it came to pass that after *this manner of language* did I *persuade* my brethren, that they might be faithful in keeping the commandments of God" (emphasis added). Nephi successfully used "language" (or persuasion) to teach others— without hesitation or apology.

Another example: "For we labor diligently to write [another way of communicating or teaching], to *persuade* our children and also our brethren to believe in Christ" (2 Nephi 25:23; emphasis added). Let's pray that your communications to friends and family back home can be equally persuasive.

How did great missionaries like Paul, Nephi, and Abinadi obtain this gift—and how can you? The scriptures have the answer (you'll discover this a lot as a missionary). In the Doctrine and Covenants, we are told: "No power or influence can or ought to be maintained by virtue of the priesthood" (D&C 121:41). In other words, you can't simply say, "I hold the priesthood, so you have to do as I say." That's not the way of the Lord. We are to "*cry* repentance," not demand it.

This verse further instructs that power and influence should be exercised "only by *persuasion*, by longsuffering [patience], by gentleness and meekness, and by love unfeigned" (D&C 121:41; emphasis added). "Workers together with him" (2 Corinthians 6:1) persuade people to come unto Jesus only with true, sincere, gentle love.

Persuading is not coming up with a great comeback for something someone might say. Disputation and debate are not a part of missionary work. You value the message of the loving Christ so much that you could never be arrogant about it. Nor do you know the answer to every question. With meekness, you communicate that just as your investigator is on the path of gospel learning, you are as well.

And don't forget longsuffering and patience. Why? Because many of the people you teach—even with your best skills, and even with the Spirit present—will still reject the gospel message. They will exercise their agency and choose to go in a different direction.

As mentioned earlier, the Book of Mormon is full of such accounts—which, by the way, gave me encouragement and hope as a missionary. For example, the faithful endurance of Alma and Amulek (see Alma, chapters 9–14) in the face of suffering encouraged me to keep trying as a missionary.

"Some who come and see will, perhaps, never join the Church," taught Elder Uchtdorf. "Some will at a later time. That is their choice. But that doesn't change our love for them. So, don't be discouraged if someone does not accept the gospel message immediately. It is not a personal failure. That is between the individual and Heavenly Father" ("Missionary Work: Share What Is in Your Heart," *Ensign*, May 2019).

Like prophets of old and today, you don't need to apologize for righteously persuading and convincing (see 2 Nephi 26:27) because those words also mean you are properly *influencing*. The truth is that you influence people every day of your life. At some time in your life, someone probably influenced you to do something you knew was right: serve a mission.

You will exercise lots of influence as a missionary. You'll influence your companion constantly. You might suggest, "Sister, let's have a prayer before we go." Or "You know what, Elder? Let's do tacos instead of hamburgers today." You influence your companion when you suggest turning down Elm Drive as opposed to Oak Street and when you propose a certain topic for companion study.

President Joseph F. Smith—one of the most gifted lecturers and writers in Church history and one of the most well-read Brethren the Church has ever known—said, "I cannot save you. You cannot save me. We cannot save each other, only so far as we can persuade each other to receive the truth by teaching it" (Conference Report, April 1902, 84).

Elders and Sisters, like every gift from God, the adversary has created counterfeits. And we need to be watchful of them. He has distorted the principle of persuasion, has infiltrated influence, and has turned noble convincing into cunning craftiness. Lucifer, the "father of all lies" (Moses 4:4), masterfully convinced, but in an unrighteous way. (What else is new? That's how he does everything.) And you know how *that* turned out: he successfully persuaded a third of the hosts of heaven to rebel against our Heavenly Father.

But Satan wasn't the only warrior in that war in heaven. God also used persuasion, righteous persuasion based on truth, to encourage us to accept a better plan. "Lucifer led a rebellion," said President Henry B. Eyring. "Jehovah's sustaining voice prevailed, and He volunteered to be our Savior. The fact that you are in mortality now assures us that you sustained the Father and the Savior" ("The Power of Sustaining Faith," *Ensign*, May 2019).

"Jehovah's sustaining voice prevailed." You were persuaded by our Father and our Elder Brother. You accepted the Plan. Here, then, is the critical thing for you to remember, especially as a missionary: God the Father and God the Son did *not* persuade you or anyone else using force or compulsion. That was Satan's ploy. In fact, it's one of two major things that made Satan's plan different (he also wanted all the glory, remember?). Righteous Jehovah, on the other hand, stepped forward and demonstrated perfect persuasion, something He learned from the Father.

Simply put, the Savior is the most influential of all of Heavenly Father's children. He teaches His followers principles that are right and just. He patiently persuades. Then each one of us is free to *voluntarily* accept or reject His message. He *never* forces anyone against his or her will. Never. Meekness won't allow it.

He is your model as a missionary: share the good news with others, and gently, lovingly persuade them to enter His better path. Then you can come closer to teaching in the Savior's way, "for his word was with power" (Luke 4:32).

The Source of Your Confidence

If missionary work sounds a little intimidating to you—and believe me, you wouldn't be alone in that—I'd like to share a scripture that should really help: "Therefore, verily I say unto you, lift up your voices unto this people; speak the thoughts that I shall put into your hearts, and you shall not be confounded before men; For it shall be given you in the very hour, yea, in the very moment, what ye shall say" (D&C 100:5–6).

It will be given to *you. You* will know what to say as you teach and try to righteously influence. You can be filled with confidence by knowing that the Spirit will give you the words you should say if you'll just open your mouth. How radical is *that?*

Before Samuel the Lamanite climbed to the top of the wall in Zarahemla to preach to the Nephites, he didn't know in advance what he was going to say. In fact, Helaman 13:3 tells us that he was told to stand on the wall until the words he should speak to the people came into his heart.

Talk about a miracle! Here he was, standing on top of a wall where everyone could see him. He might as well have had a target on his chest. And *he didn't even know what he was going to say.* But he did have faith. He knew the Lord would inspire him—would put the right words into his heart. And those would be the words he would teach.

Remember, too, that this was a rough crowd—"they cast stones at him upon the wall, and also many shot arrows at him as he stood upon the wall." But the Spirit of the Lord "was with him, insomuch that they could not hit him with their stones neither with their arrows" (Helaman 16:2).

And guess what? The same thing can happen to you (figuratively, of course).

But wait just a minute. Do you think Samuel confidently scaled that wall without having spent considerable time studying the gospel? No way. He may not have known what he was going to say, but he knew a whole lot about the doctrine and the principles and the prophecies.

Do you think Samuel climbed that wall without having lived the gospel he was teaching? Nope. The testimony he boldly shared at the risk of his life came from living it every day and seeing its positive impact.

The same thing applies to you. You cannot confidently stand on the wall waiting for God to speak through you if you haven't done your part by studying the gospel. You cannot sit in a missionary lesson believing that God will simply tell you what to say if you haven't done the work ahead of time. The Lord won't draw from an empty well. You need to fill your well with a) study, b) prayer, and c) righteous living.

The Lord expects—and even requires—you to develop knowledge and an understanding of His gospel before He'll give you "in the very hour, yea, in the very moment, what ye shall say." Here's what else He will do: if you've prepared by studying and if you've been obedient and exact in living the gospel to the best of your ability, He'll remind you of what you've studied and lived. He'll bring those truths to your memory. Through your constant companion, the Spirit, He'll put those feelings in your heart and those words into your mouth so you can teach them. And He'll do it in the very moment you need them.

Among the many lessons we can learn from the life of Oliver Cowdery, one of this dispensation's early leaders, is that you can't simply ask for something and expect to get it. You have to study it out first. You can't just "take no thought save it was to ask" (D&C 9:7).

"Studying it out" means you open the scriptures, then learn and practice the principles. And for you as a missionary, it also means you practice the skills of teaching those principles. Then, after all that (after "all we can do" [2 Nephi 25:23]), the Lord will put exact ideas and thoughts into your heart and into your mind. That's how it works: you do your part to prepare, and, like the sons of Mosiah, He will use you as an effective instrument to teach His gospel (see Mosiah 17:36).

You're told that "The Spirit will draw upon the knowledge and skills you have developed to help you teach more powerfully" (*Preach My Gospel*, 178). Read that carefully. It tells you that the Spirit needs you to first *develop* knowledge and skills before He can draw on what you have gained.

You're also told that others will be influenced "by how well you explain the gospel" (*Preach My Gospel*, 178). If you want to explain it, you have to know it—and that's a major reason for individual and companion study. It's a real reason to live what you teach.

Now, not only will you need to explain the gospel, but it must be done in a way that people can understand. President John Taylor said, "It is true intelligence for a man to take a subject that is mysterious and great in itself, and to unfold and simplify it so that a child can understand it" (*The Gospel Kingdom*, sel. G. Homer Durham [Salt Lake City: Bookcraft, 1943], 270; *Preach My Gospel*, 184). Did you catch that? One of the greatest gifts you can have as a missionary is the ability to help those who are new to the gospel understand the gospel language, simply.

I know that as you prepare, as you put in the effort, and as you live the gospel, you will be blessed with the confidence you need to approach, assess, teach, and testify to the people of the world.

You've been promised that the Lord will help you lift up your voice (see D&C 100:5–6).

To qualify for that incredible blessing, you need to develop the skills of speaking and teaching. Work to improve your talents. Commit to take the time to develop good habits.

Maybe you grew up in the Church and the gospel principles you've learned are part of you. They're second nature. Your confidence may come from years—even a lifetime—of learning. Whether you have that foundation or you're just now starting to study in earnest, put your entire heart into mastering the teaching skills you'll find on these pages. You can't wave a magic wand and get those skills overnight—but if you absorb them over time and if you *practice, practice, practice,* I promise you will become a more articulate, confident, and effective teacher of the things you know to be true.

Chapter Two

What to Know Before Saying a Word

"What *we* are interested in . . . usually isn't what
***others* are interested in. Others typically want**
the *results* of the doctrine, not the doctrine."

President Dallin H. Oaks,
"Sharing the Restored Gospel," *Ensign*, November 2016

People. You'll meet a lot of them as a missionary.

How will you get their attention? Back in the day, missionaries used to attract attention by standing on objects in the street and singing or preaching at the top of their lungs. They got lots of attention, all right—sometimes not the kind they wanted.

Fortunately, there is an easier way. Do this and you'll be a more skilled teacher—or, put another way, a more effective missionary:

Figure out what people want and show them how to get it through the gospel of Jesus Christ.

Think about those who will cross your path as you serve. Some have never shown (and might never show) an interest in hearing the gospel. There will be new investigators. There will be "eternal" investigators. There will be those who are already receiving the lessons or who have recently been baptized. Add to that all the Church members you will come to know in your assigned branches, wards, districts, and stakes.

That's a pretty diverse collection of people. But here's the cool part: They all want the same things.

That's right. If you were to poll people of all races, nationalities, and socioeconomic backgrounds, and ask them what two things they want more of in life, they would say *time* and *money*.

People Want More Time

Okay, let's not take this literally. I mean, who wants a longer Monday? (Well, maybe missionaries do if that's their P-day.) When people say they want more time, what they *really* want is to spend more of the time they have on the things and people that are most important to them.

Let's agree, then, that what people are really saying is they want more *quality time*.

Quality time involves doing what they find most fulfilling, rewarding, and memorable.

Quality time is the time they spend with the people and things they care most about, which could include family, friends, associates, colleagues, fellow Church members, interests, and leisure activities.

People Want More Money

Everyone wants enough money to take care of their needs. Most would also like enough to enjoy some of the extras.

But there's a problem. There are only a few *legal* ways (other than scoring a huge inheritance) to get more money. One is to work harder. The other is to work longer.

And what does either do to the amount of quality time that's left for someone to spend with the people and things they value most? You got it—quality time takes it on the chin because now they're spending more of their time at work.

So, we have a dilemma: time and money—the two things everyone claims they want more of—seem contradictory. There are always those stunning exceptions, but it appears *most* people can't reasonably have both simultaneously.

That's where you as a missionary come in. No, you won't be passing out wads of cash to people or slowing down the revolution of the earth. But you *will* be able to help them understand that those two universal wants—time and money—are both possible through the gospel of Jesus Christ as they learn from you what they *really* mean.

Quality Time = Achieving Objectives

Let's take a deeper dive into the first one, *quality time*. We'll get to *more money* a little bit later.

To explain what quality time really means, let's begin by looking at a simple word that should be well understood by every missionary. The word is *objective*. (Note: not *objection*. Yes, you'll hear those just about every day, but we'll cover those in detail a few chapters from now.)

Everyone has objectives, even if they don't *call* them objectives. So, here's what you need to remember: if you can help people understand and meet their objectives, you give them a compelling reason to listen to you and to ultimately accept the gospel.

A little exercise will help you see what I mean. Get a blank piece of paper. (I'm serious about this—if you'll go along with me here, it will be very helpful later on.) Across the top, write **Daily Objectives**. Now, below that, draw vertical lines to create three equal columns across the page. In this exercise, you're going to consider three groups of people: children, single adults, and couples/parents.

Let's label the first column **Children**.

The following might seem like a real stretch, but go with it: think about what eight- to eighteen-year-olds might have as daily objectives. (It's true: even a ten-year-old kid has objectives. They may call them "things I wanna do" or "stuff I want.") Do a little mental role-playing and come up with the things this age group wants to accomplish or have in a day. But don't think about just material things; consider the mental, intellectual, social, and spiritual side of kids. As you do, jot each one down—no more than a word or two or three per objective— and either number or bullet them down the page.

You might write things like:

• Have fun
• Be entertained

- Eat good food
- Make friends
- No fighting (harmony)
- Popularity (activities and school)
- Get compliments
- Good grades
- Feel important
- Relax (hang out)
- Date (acceptance)
- Independence

Obviously, an eight-year-old will have different objectives than a sixteen-year-old, but you get the idea. And certainly, if we brought a bunch of kids from this age group together and asked them to review my list or the one you make on your own, they'd probably re-prioritize them to their own liking—which is fine.

But here's the question I'd ask as you look over the list (and you should try to have fifteen to twenty objectives for this and each column): Is there anything on this list that a typical eight- to eighteen-year old would find unimportant, unnecessary, or irrelevant to their daily life? I'm going to guess that the answer is probably *no.*

Okay, then. Let's go on to the middle column.

Label the middle column **Single Adults**. This one won't take a lot of mental role-playing, because as a missionary, you fall into this group. You know the kinds of things important to you and your friends. In this category, you might write things like:

- Employment
- Skills development
- Positive relationships
- Networking
- Academic/professional achievement
- Acknowledgment or recognition
- Improve physical appearance
- Enjoy hobbies
- Fitness
- Entertainment

Again, a single nineteen-year-old will probably have different objectives than a single twenty-nine-year-old or a divorced thirty-eight-year-old, but jot down everything you can think of. Remember, you're not making an exhaustive list—you're trying to identify stuff that's common to most. When you're done, ask the same question: is there anything on this list that a typical single adult would find unimportant, unnecessary, or irrelevant to his or her daily life? I suppose the answer again will be *no, it all looks pretty important, necessary, and relevant to singles.* Let's go, then, to the right side of your page.

At the top of the last column, write **Couples/Parents**. These are adults who are or who have been married. It's a broad category that includes everyone from newlyweds to a father of six to a widowed grandmother of nineteen. This will call for more mental role-playing as you think about what would be important to this group. I suppose you might write things like:

- Financial security
- Ensuring safety
- Purpose
- Love and support
- Respect
- Service
- Leaving a legacy
- Establishing traditions
- Peace
- Stability

If you get stuck, think about your older siblings, parents, grandparents, and their friends—what do you think they're trying to accomplish in life? After you complete a list of your own (go ahead and borrow from any that I've listed), ask yourself the same question: is there anything on this list that a typical couple or parent would find unimportant, unnecessary, or irrelevant to their daily life?

Now, just because we chose these three particular audiences doesn't mean you shouldn't stretch this exercise further on your own. You and your companion might make columns for the kind of people that you encounter most often. For example, if there's a retirement community in your area, create a list of daily objectives for empty nesters or retirees. Don't worry about trying to get the objectives in perfect order, because you never will. Everyone's unique and would prioritize them differently. The important thing is that you have some well-thought-out lists from which you can work.

All right, so what's the point of this exercise? As a missionary, you will work with all three of these groups—I call them target audiences. At some homes, you'll find all three categories of people. And with these lists, you have just identified that which matters most to the people you will teach. These are the things that motivate them and inspire them to get up every morning, the things that, when accomplished, help them sleep well at night. These are the things that give people reason to live. These objectives are what they think about and hope for each day.

Why does that matter to you as a missionary? Because with very few exceptions, these daily objectives can be found and achieved through the gospel of Jesus Christ! Your message, the good news you have been called to share—the gospel plan, the doctrines you teach—all involve the most important things people live for.

The people you meet have wants and needs. *You have the answers.*

Let's consider that for a minute. How many times do missionaries introduce themselves and their message as something different from—or even inconsistent with—someone's daily objectives? How many times do missionaries immediately hit someone up with, "Have you ever heard of the Book of Mormon?"

Let's be candid. First, you and I agree that the Book of Mormon is the most incredible book ever given to mankind. It's a book the Prophet Joseph Smith described as "the most correct of any book on earth, and the keystone of our religion, and a man would get nearer to God by abiding by its precepts, than by any other book" (History of the Church, 4:461).

But what about people who have never heard of the Book of Mormon? I guarantee it's not on their "daily objectives" list. In fact, it's such a foreign concept to them that if you lead out with that question, they'll likely say something like, "You know, I don't have time to read a book" (*especially* a 531-page mega-book). They might quickly decide a 531-page book won't fit into their hectic schedule. No wonder they'll say something like, "I don't really think you can find true happiness from a book" (hint: happiness could be their top objective right now). Or they could give this quick comeback: "I believe in the Bible, and that's all we really need."

When you lead out with the Book of Mormon, you've offered them a *product*. Think about that. A "product" isn't why people get up every morning. Someone who knows little or nothing about the Church didn't get up this morning with the sole intent to read the Book of Mormon. In fact, how many people around the world—really—got up this morning and said to themselves, "Boy, I sure hope someone gives me a free five-hundred-page religious book today."⬚

Sadly, no. That person probably got up this morning and said, "I've gotta figure out how to create more peace in our family. There's so much arguing and contention right now. This is the third day in a row I've left for work after fighting with my wife. We just can't seem to get on the same page anymore. Nothing I do or say makes her happy. It's killing me. I don't know how this is going end."

Rather than focus on a book—or any other "product"—figure out how to focus your message on what that person is looking for. I love how President Oaks described this teaching principle:

> As we speak to others, we need to remember that an invitation to learn more about Jesus Christ and His gospel is preferable to an invitation to learn more about our Church. We want people to be converted to the gospel. That is the great role of the Book of Mormon. Feelings about our Church follow conversion to Jesus Christ; they do not precede it. Many who are suspicious of churches nevertheless have a love for the Savior. Put first things first. ("Sharing the Restored Gospel," *Ensign*, November 2016)

If I can interject, then, what I interpret President Oaks to be saying is that if we begin our communication with investigators talking about a product—such as the Church, modern-day prophets, the Word of Wisdom, temples, and so forth—we are opening ourselves up to objections. And what missionary wants that?

As much as we have learned to revere and love modern-day prophets and temples and everything else associated with the Church, to someone unfamiliar with the gospel or the workings of the Spirit, those things, at first, are products. Contrary to what Elder Uchtdorf and Elder Bednar counseled us (see p. 17), we're now coming across as a salesperson peddling a bunch of products. "Do you want a book? No? How 'bout a program for families on Monday nights? Or a guide to staying healthier that includes eating more herbs? If that doesn't sound good, we're starting a yoga class for moms on Tuesday morning at our building. . . ."

It doesn't matter what good our programs might bring—until people have felt the Spirit and begun to trust who you are and the best in life that you represent, they're going to find your offerings objectionable. *I don't like history. I work on Monday nights. I don't need to lose weight. I hate yoga.* There are objections to every product.

What should you do instead? Not to sound too dramatic, but here's the answer that could change your entire mission experience:

Don't focus on the Church or any of its "products." Focus on the *results* the Church of Jesus Christ and His gospel bring!

Mind if I say that again?

Don't focus on the Church or any of its "products." Focus on the *results* the Church of Jesus Christ and His gospel bring!

Results is the word of the day. It's even better than *objectives*. You see, everyone starts the day with an objective. That's great. But they know it's been a good—maybe a great—day if they've achieved results. And the objectives you listed on that paper should now be termed *results*.

Let's go back to that man who's fighting with his wife every morning. He's looking for a particular result as he backs out of the driveway: peace and harmony in his home. He's hoping for that same result as he pulls into the garage that evening. Will Jesus Christ help him with that? Will the Savior's Church and His word as found in scriptures help him achieve it? Yes, yes, and yes!

Focus on the result he wants first, then he'll be more open to learning *how* to achieve that result. In time—when the time is right—you'll be able to introduce the Book of Mormon to him. You *know* the answers he needs are found in that book, and you're positive it's a tool he can use to overcome his challenge. He will come to realize that, too, once he gains confidence that you understand the results he desires.

When speaking of our friends and investigators and how and when to introduce certain gospel principles to them, President Oaks instructed further, "They may also be interested when they are seeking more happiness [a result], closeness to God [a result], or a better understanding of the purpose of life [a result]" (Dallin H. Oaks, "Sharing the Gospel," *Ensign*, Nov. 2016; bracketed words added).

In time and with the Spirit's guidance, you will always find the right moment to introduce the Book of Mormon and other core elements of the gospel. But the first thing you must do is ask yourself, ***What might this person be trying to accomplish today that the gospel can provide? And how can I address that daily result so he'll see that I've got answers and solutions for him?***

Hopefully this is making sense to you. (I'm trying to reason with you here.) Let me share three quick but significant examples to further demonstrate this principle.

You remember the story of Ammon (see Alma 17:18–19:36). Though he was chief among the sons of Mosiah, his humble approach to teaching the gospel didn't involve "pushing product." In fact, when he entered the Lamanite land of Ishmael, he basically said, "I want to work for you, King Lamoni, and I may just remain your servant until the day I die." Rather than talk about baptism immediately, he served the person who he prayed would someday become his investigator (not to mention all who worked for him—in fact, Lamoni's entire kingdom).

By focusing on results that he believed were important to Lamoni (respect, managing his lands, trustworthy servants), "king Lamoni was much pleased with Ammon" (Alma 17:24). Ammon not only won his trust, but also the following of an entire Lamanite kingdom. Many souls were thus saved.

Meanwhile (example #2), over in another Lamanite land called Jerusalem, Ammon's brother Aaron got right to work (see Alma 21), entering the synagogue there and telling everyone he had seen an angel and that they must repent, and so on. Fair to say, it didn't go over too well. He got into some pretty heated arguments over scriptures and resurrection and other important gospel truths. "And they contended with many about the word" (Alma 21:11).

When that didn't go as planned, Aaron decided to transfer himself to Middoni. But his approach was basically the same. No attention paid to the results people wanted, only the topics Aaron wanted to talk about. And, what do you know? He got thrown into prison. (Later, his results-oriented brother Ammon had to bail him out.)

Now, that's not to say the doctrines Aaron was trying to teach were wrong, but as President Oaks said, "What *we* are interested in, like the important additional doctrinal teachings in the restored Church, usually isn't what *others* are interested in. Others typically want the *results* of the doctrine, not the doctrine" ("Sharing the Restored Gospel," *Ensign*, November 2016). Apparently, Aaron did not put "first things first."

Example #3: What is one of the most quoted verses in latter-day scripture? It is the voice of the Lord as found in Moses 1:39: "For behold, this is my work and my glory—to bring to pass the immortality and eternal life of man." This is God speaking about His ultimate result. He wants us to achieve immortality and eternal life. Before He tells us the *how*, He makes clear the *what*.

In other words, before He teaches the doctrine, He makes clear the result we can achieve through the doctrine. Before He instructs us on ordinances, He makes sure we understand the purpose of the

ordinances. And before He introduces the Church and all its marvelous administrative programs and policies, He wants us to always keep
our eye on the prize—the ultimate result of immortality and eternal
life.

Now, can you see how remaining locked on the *results* the gospel
brings will not only be more interesting and personable and relevant
to your investigators, it will also be more aligned with how the Lord
would have you preach His gospel?

How Will I Know?

I get it if right about now you're asking yourself how you can
possibly know which of the many objectives/results you've considered is the right one for the person you're approaching. Fair question.
Luckily, the answer is easier than you might think.

First, rely on the Spirit. That is your single greatest tool in figuring
out what to address. Discovering and addressing a person's objectives
fits right in with the way the Brethren want you to teach the gospel.
Back in the day, missionaries had to memorize and recite specific discussions and teach concepts in a certain order. Today, above all, the
Brethren trust that you will follow the Spirit. Elder Neil L. Andersen
said, "As you respond to spiritual promptings, the Holy Ghost will
carry your words to the heart of another" ("A Witness of God," *Ensign*,
November 2016). You will know what results to bring up.

Second, after studying it out in your mind, simply make an edu-
cated assumption. You've done that to a large degree in the exercise
when you identified common objectives. And don't forget, at the end of
each column I challenged you to ask this simple question: Are any of
these objectives/results unimportant, unnecessary, or irrelevant to this
type of person? The answer was most likely, "No." That should give you
confidence that while you may not know a person's hottest button
on that certain day, you can make an inspired guess as to something
that is at least important, necessary, or relevant, in some way or
another, in his or her life.

Finally, ask yourself, *Is this objective something the gospel helps someone achieve?* If it is and you can introduce it in a rational way, using appropriate reasoning, you're prepared to craft a better introduction for the person you meet. (More on that later.)

When you do this, you're speaking to people in their native language (and I'm not talking Mandarin Chinese or Portuguese). I'm talking the language they understand in their heart. You're no longer speaking a language they'll instantly perceive as strange, offensive, threatening—or worse. Might this be part of speaking the "language of the Lord"? Of course. Did He not know the intents and desires of people's hearts?

Once you've identified and discussed what's most important to someone, you can then introduce the appropriate tools the Church provides to help that person—yes, the Book of Mormon, and possibly the Children and Youth program, the family home evening program, the self-reliance program, or the temple and family history program, to name a few. Knowing what's most important to a person will help you introduce the right tool or program at the right time.

This way of approaching people and families not only shows how the gospel can touch every facet of life and help people achieve daily results, but it also helps you "get in the door" as you seek people to teach. That's because they will more readily understand how the gospel applies to their life and will help them achieve the things most important to them.

And here's the best part. Only a few messages, products, or services in the world deliver the results they promise. For achieving universally applicable daily results, I believe that there is no greater message than the restored gospel of Jesus Christ.

Turning the Principle into Practice

Let's look at a few specific examples of how this results-first approach can work. Imagine a parent has the objective of providing for his family. Can that objective be achieved through the gospel? Sure can—in many ways. One is the law of tithing. So, do you knock on the door and say, "Hi! We came to your house today to tell you about living the law of tithing, which includes contributing 10 percent of your increase to our Church."

Uh, no. You'd probably be laughed—or maybe thrown—off the doorstep.

Instead of talking first about the product—the law of tithing—address how important you know it is for parents to provide for their family. Once he agrees that providing for his family is a daily pursuit, you've shown that you understand him. You've also started an agreeable conversation where you can explain how the gospel can help him provide for his family. And he's more likely to accept what you say.

Don't get me wrong. He's not about to say, "Wow! That's amazing! You know just what I'm trying to do every single day. Get in here and teach me!" But he will likely be thinking, *This is a perceptive person. This person understands what I'm looking for, even though I'm twice his age. Even though he's from Idaho and I'm from Boston. Even though we just met, he's talking about something relevant to me.*

What about a person who you perceive to be concerned with raising kids in today's world? After you find common ground that this is a daily concern parents share, you can eventually describe how our prophets have emphasized a family-centered, Church-supported way of worshipping.

These modern prophets, you can further explain, have given amazing guidance and resources on how families can become stronger—inside and outside the home—as more segments of society attempt to weaken and even destroy the family unit. The inspired Brethren have not only warned and admonished us to be watchful, but they've provided numerous tools for families to stay strong and be protected from the enticements of the world.

Look again at the lists you made in the three columns. Ask yourself which results are realistically *not* attainable through the gospel or Church. Examples might be "being entertained" or "being more popular at school." If something can't reasonably be attained using the gospel, I'd recommend not using it as an approach. Remove it from the list.

What About Wanting More Money?

Earlier I said that the two things in life most people claim they want—having more quality time and getting more money—didn't really work together. But you'll remember I changed *quality time* to *daily results*.

Next, I'm going to suggest another word change, this time for the second desire in life. Instead of the word *money*, a more accurate word is *prosperity*.

Prosperity isn't limited to financial wealth. In fact, *prosperity* comes from the Latin word meaning "according to one's hope." In Hebrew, *prosperity* means to be unified with God. It seems that over the centuries we've turned a truly noble pursuit into a worldly passion. True prosperity comes from pursuing a life of happiness, purpose, and meaning.

Prosperity can be defined in many ways. You can be prosperous in your relationships. You can be prosperous at work. You can be prosperous in your community. You can have a prosperous family. In short, as it says many times in scripture, you can "prosper in the land" (as just a few examples, see 2 Nephi 1:20; Jarom 1:9; Mosiah 10:5; Alma 9:13; Alma 50:20; Helaman 3:20).

Prosperity can include financial wealth, but it goes far beyond that. When you achieve it, prosperity means success in many other areas of your life and the joy of having the presence of God with you. So *that* truly is one of the two things most people want in life.

I'm pleased to report, prosperity and quality time are *not* contradictory, after all. Instead, they are very complimentary ideas.

Yet, lest we think we can have it all to ourselves, President Russell M. Nelson had something to say about these two things we all desire. He taught the need for us to give a portion of both back to the Lord:

"Think of this: In paying tithing, we return one-tenth of our increase to the Lord. In keeping the Sabbath holy, we reserve one day in seven as His. So it is our privilege to consecrate both money and time to Him who lends us life each day" ("The Sabbath Is a Delight," *Ensign*, May 2015).

As I see it—and hopefully as you'll teach it—living the gospel of Jesus Christ will not only provide us more quality time and prosperity with those we love, it will actually expand our capacity to receive those blessings. So much, in fact, that returning to the Father a tenth of the increase He's given us and one of every seven days He allows us to be on this earth will only enhance the possibility of receiving even more!

Most people don't know that the keys to quality time and prosperity are found in the gospel of Jesus Christ. That's why they say "no" to our message. But in their premortal lives they knew and accepted this truth. They have just forgotten. That's why they're here on earth—so that a messenger can remind them.

You are the messenger. "And how shall they believe in him [and His gospel] of whom they have not heard? And how shall they hear without a preacher? And how shall they preach, except they be sent?" (Romans 10:14–15 [bracketed words added]).

Go and bring to their memory the two important things they came to earth to obtain: quality time with those they love, eternally; and prosperity (unity with God) forever!

Chapter Three

Principles for Proclaiming

**"We desire to be more effective in fulfilling our
divinely appointed responsibility to proclaim
the restored gospel in all the world."**

President Dallin H. Oaks,
"Sharing the Restored Gospel," *Ensign*, November 2016

With a sound understanding of what drives and motivates Heavenly
Father's children, the best teachers—missionaries—act on these four
principles to make their work powerful and effective:

1. **Focus on results.**
2. **Do what successful missionaries do.**
3. **Don't distract from the Spirit.**
4. **Proclaim the gospel with urgency.**

Principle 1: Focus on Results

Regarding the exercise you did in the last chapter—where you
brainstormed daily objectives for people in three different groups: grab
that paper again. If you haven't done it already, cross out *Objectives* at
the top and in its place write *Results*. (Go along with me here—you'll
see why as you read through this section.)

Results is a word that will serve you well, and I encourage you to
use it often in your planning and teaching. Here's a glimpse of how it
works: Think and talk about the results your investigators are seeking.

As you work with your companion, ask, "What is the Peterson family trying to achieve? What is the number-one result they are striving to obtain as a family right now? Is it health, peace, togetherness, unity, legacy?" Once you've studied it and prayed about it, you'll know how to better approach them and which doctrine or gospel principle to share in order to truly speak their language.

As a missionary, focus on results in everything you provide. Don't focus on products or programs or processes. Don't decide you're going to pass out twenty Books of Mormon that day, even if a natural disaster strikes. Don't decide you're going to get fifteen people to tour the Family History Center—or die trying. A missionary focused on products instead of results is one who focuses only on numbers, who measures success only by statistics, who hammers on products, programs, and processes.

Elder Neil L. Andersen counseled new mission presidents and their wives at the 2016 Seminar for New Mission Presidents at the MTC in Provo, Utah, that the pendulum of convert baptisms, when too aggressively emphasized and promoted without proper context, can swing too far to one side, causing baptism without repentance and an overemphasis on numbers.

As a missionary, if you rivet your attention on results, baptisms will not be your chief focus. If it is, you're focusing only on a process. Instead, you focus on *the results baptism brings,* which include such blessings as repentance, forgiveness, newness of life, and closeness to God.

Obviously, baptism is a necessity. We all know that. We testify of it. It's clearly stated in the scriptures. (See, for example, Alma 9:27; D&C 20:25, 112:29.) But the question of when it is properly addressed is my point.

I follow the Savior's order of things. When He appeared to the Nephites, the first command He gave to Nephi and the newly called Twelve was this: "Verily I say unto you, that whoso repenteth of his sins *through your words,* and desireth to be baptized in my name, on this wise shall ye baptize them" (3 Nephi 11:23; emphasis added). You see, "words," or the preaching of the gospel and its attendant results, came first. The ordinance followed.

When you introduce the gospel to someone, it's unlikely that person is going to have the same background or knowledge about baptism that you have. Therefore, it's not wise to focus on baptism right off the bat. Preparing for baptism can be a lengthy or a short process, but it is still a process. It's a tool that enables a person to receive something greater. And that something greater is probably found on the list of results they are seeking.

Programs—like products—can also be objectionable to investigators. Programs of the Church can even be off-putting. That doesn't mean they're not worth our while. They are. That doesn't mean they're not inspired. They are! I know that, and you know that. But a brand-new investigator may not get that right away. She *will*, though, respond to something that gets her the results she wants.

How might an investigator respond if you try to convince him to hold family home evening (a product, program, or process) before you know what results are most important to him? He'll likely say, "I can't do that since, uh, you know, Monday night is my football night."

Or what if you try to sell a woman on service in the Church before you've figured out the results she wants? She's going to respond, "You know what, um, this whole idea about 'callings,' that's probably not going to work for me. I'm busy enough at work, and I already volunteer at the school."

If you bypass results, you're going to get objections. Every time. You make it easy for people to reject your message.

Let's take a look at some examples of how this works. Imagine you give a new investigator the Book of Mormon without making any effort to find out what that investigator needs or wants. You put the book in her hands and say, "I want you to read this book. We'll be back in a few days to see how you're coming along with it."

What's she going to say? "I don't have the time." "I'm not a very good reader." "I do audiobooks." "I already have my Bible."

Now imagine you approach that same person and say, "We'd like to suggest a way for your family to enjoy greater peace every day." Who's going to tell you they don't need more peace? How many are going to say, "Oh, c'mon, that's nonsense"? No one can reasonably object to having more peace. It's something all of us want! Remember?

Or how about approaching someone and saying:

"We'd like to share with you a way to gain even more confidence that a loving Heavenly Father knows you and will look after you every day—no matter what you're experiencing."

How many people are going to respond with, "No thanks, I don't need that"? Sure—you might encounter the odd exception. But I'm not talking about exceptions. I'm trying to share general rules of effective teaching that you can adapt to almost any situation.

If you'll approach people with results rather than products, results rather than processes, you will find that it becomes very hard for them to reject you (or the Lord, who you represent).

Regarding the saving ordinance of baptism, what are some of the results one gets from being baptized? In his signature way, listen how Elder Dieter F. Uchtdorf gently teaches this principle as he speaks to our friends and neighbors:

> If you sense that your life could have more meaning [a result], a higher purpose [a result], stronger family bonds [definitely a result], and a closer connection with God [another result], please, come, join us.
>
> If you seek a community of people who are working to become the best versions of themselves [a result], help those in need [a result], and make this world a better place [big result!], come, join us! ("Your Great Adventure," *Ensign*, November 2019; bracketed expressions added)

Along with these and other results suggested earlier, if someone wants fellowship with people who are just like them, who are going through the same life challenges as they are, *then* you can teach how baptism produces that result.

Is fellowship and acceptance objectionable? No. That's exactly what anyone would want. And if you can show the investigator how to get that, do you think she's going to say, "Oh, that's crazy talk"?

What if someone wants to overcome habits and addictions that have weighed him down for the last ten years? What if freedom from addiction or a new lease on life is the result he wants? You can show him how he can discard bad habits or weaknesses and start over through a wonderful ordinance called baptism. How many people in that position are going to say, "Not interested"? Very, very few.

Instead of talking to your investigators about baptism, *talk about the results they will receive from baptism.* That's a powerful way to open dialogue, because you're starting every conversation with something that's agreeable rather than objectionable—and objections usually lead to rejections.

You'll find the importance of focusing on results in the scriptures. Check out this brilliant illustration of missionaries who focused on results:

> Yea, and there was continual peace among them, and exceedingly great prosperity in the church because of their heed and diligence which they gave unto the word of God, which was declared unto them by Helaman, and Shiblon, and Corianton, and Ammon and his brethren, yea, and by all those who had been ordained by the holy order of God, being baptized unto repentance, and sent forth to preach among the people. (Alma 49:30)

What was happening to the people of Nephi? There was "continual peace among them"—another way of saying they enjoyed quality time. There was also "exceedingly great prosperity"—one of those things everyone wishes they had more of.

Why did they have those things? Because of the heed and diligence they gave the word of God, "which was declared unto them by Helaman, and Shiblon, and Corianton, and Ammon and his brethren, yea, and by all those who had been ordained by the holy order of God . . . and sent forth to preach among the people." Those missionaries were successful because they were results-focused teachers who helped the Nephites achieve the results of peace and great prosperity.

They didn't focus on product. They didn't focus on process. They focused on results.

Want another illustration from the scriptures? When Alma the Elder baptized the penitent at the waters of Mormon (see Mosiah 18), I doubt he talked about the process (mechanics) of baptism as much as the result they would get from it. He didn't say, "Okay, when we go into the water, I'm gonna put my hand right here. You put your hand on my wrist. Now, plug your nose, and you've gotta make sure we get everything under the water, 'cause if we don't, we're gonna have to do it all over again." No. While that's obviously a vital consideration, I don't think that was Alma the Elder's primary concern. His primary concern was helping the people achieve the results they sought.

In Mosiah 18:8–10, Alma talked about the results his people would receive by making the baptismal commitment. Pay attention to his words:

> And now, as ye are desirous to come into the fold of God [*that is one result they wanted*], and to be called his people [*this is another*], . . . that ye may be redeemed of God [*a third result*], and be numbered with those of the first resurrection [*yet another result*] that ye may have eternal life [*a fifth result identified*]—Now I say unto you, if this be the desire of your hearts, what have you against being baptized in the name of the Lord? (Bracketed emphasis added)

Do you see the pattern? Alma discussed results first—coming into the fold of God, being called His people, being redeemed of God, rising in the first resurrection, and having eternal life. *Then* he explained the tool or process by which those results would be achieved: proper baptism.

And look what happened. The people confirmed that these were indeed the results they were looking for. "And now when the people had heard these words, they clapped their hands for joy, and exclaimed: This is the desire of our hearts" (Mosiah 18:11).

No wonder Alma brought so many into the waters of baptism, gave so many that saving ordinance. First and foremost, he understood the aspiration of their hearts—the results they longed for.

Principle 2: Do What Successful Missionaries Do

The second principle for becoming the best teacher—the best missionary—is to emulate (imitate) successful missionaries. Act the way successful missionaries act. Dress the way successful missionaries dress. Speak the way successful missionaries speak. Study the way successful missionaries study. Pray and love and show patience the way successful missionaries do.

To understand what I'm getting at here, I want you to think about a teacher—in school, in church, or in some other setting—who inspired or motivated you. Consider the attributes of that person. How did that teacher get and hold your attention? What were the traits of that effective teacher? Wouldn't be a bad idea to write these down.

Think about the best seminary teacher you had, the best teacher at Especially for Youth, or your favorite instructor in Sunday School, in a priesthood quorum, or in Young Women. That person is an example of the type of teacher you need to become as a minister of the Lord. That teacher's attributes can become your attributes.

The teachers you admire may be twice your age, and your life experiences may seem to pale in comparison to theirs, but you've been set apart to become the same type of person—and you have the potential to achieve just that. The Lord has great expectations of all those who have been set apart to teach His message. If He has blessed those teachers you admire, just think how he wants to bless those whom He calls to serve full-time!

The teachers who had the greatest influence on you likely had at least some of the attributes the great philosopher Aristotle identified way back in the day—around 330 BC—as being the major qualities of effective teaching and persuasion (they're discussed on the next page). And they are the same attributes you'll find in the most effective missionaries.

It's not "fake it till you make it." It's "emulate it till you make it."

Let's look at some of the characteristics of model teachers that missionaries have shared with me.

Understanding. A successful missionary understands where someone else is coming from. Obviously, it's difficult to do that if you haven't really walked in their shoes. For example, you can't fully understand an alcohol addiction if you haven't had one. But the Lord has given you, as an ordained minister, the ability to empathize. Empathizing *doesn't* mean you necessarily agree with a person's world views or you adopt his values. Empathy simply means that you can better comprehend his thinking and perspective.

The Apostle Paul knew that in order to get the attention of those he taught, he needed to demonstrate a level of empathy. He did this by a) speaking in their Hebrew tongue and by b) letting them know he "got" their religiosity because of his own prior devoutness to Judaism before converting to Christ (see Acts 22:2–3). The Lord gives His missionaries the gift of understanding and a measure of discernment, helping you relate to others. And by relating to others, you'll learn to understand them better—and they you.

Like a chameleon (those amazing lizards that change colors to fit in with their surroundings), seek help in adapting your style and message to the personalities of those you teach so they feel they are understood and fit in. That's good teaching.

Interest. Effective teachers and good missionaries are sincerely interested in their investigators and the daily concerns of those people. These missionaries are the ones who make an unexpected phone call at 9:00 p.m. to check in on how someone is doing. These missionaries follow the promptings of the Spirit to go by an investigator's home and check on their progress, even without an appointment.

As was said by his successor about President Thomas S. Monson, "For decades he has taken the long way home, following promptings of the Spirit to arrive on someone's doorstep and then hear words such as, 'How did you know it was the anniversary of our daughter's death?' or 'How did you know it was my birthday'" (Russell M. Nelson, "The Price of Priesthood Power," *Ensign*, May 2016). These missionaries are sincere in caring about the people they teach.

Determination. A good teacher is determined to give his best for the sake of others. *Determination* in the missionary context is a gentle, diligent commitment to persistently help your investigators (and fellow ward missionaries!) reach daily objectives with enthusiasm and vigor.

It's an infectious drive for making sure your investigator understands the principle or concept. If a determined missionary doesn't think an investigator "got it," she says to her companion, "You know what? I think we need to consider another way of teaching that principle. The approach we used didn't connect with Brother Doty. Our example didn't work. He didn't relate to that scriptural reference. Let's figure out another way, or find another scripture, to make sure he's connecting with this gospel principle."

The people you teach will appreciate that you express concern, are sensitive to their thinking, help them understand, and are determined to make sure their conversion journey is joyous.

Energy. Along with determination comes energy. As a good missionary, you should be energetic about preaching the gospel! You should love your message so much that you can't wait to share it with more people. Because you appreciate and are grateful for what the gospel has done for you and your family, and what it will do for your posterity, you want others to experience that same joy along the covenant path. I can attest that the happiest days of my mission were when I "left it all out on the field"—the mission field—spending all my energy on the work.

Worth. A successful instructor sees the worth in everyone she teaches. An effective missionary lets each investigator know by his or her actions that *I don't have anything more important to do right now than to speak with you. This is my most important task of the day. I'm happy to give up everything else I have to do—my personal time, even my dinner appointment.* To convey that to a student of the gospel will build a relationship and form a connection between you and that person that may last forever.

Learning. Every great teacher is a great *learner*. If you want to effectively teach the gospel, you need to learn and know and understand and grow in the gospel yourself. A closely related attribute is this: great leaders are great followers. Leaders of the Church—our General Authorities, your mission president and his wife, and the many other leaders in your mission and your home ward and stake— are wonderful followers of the Savior.

But most of all, Jesus Christ, our Leader, was the best example of this. He followed the Father and learned from Him. Do you not think that His prayers were humble supplications to learn what the Father would have Him do? "And in the day time he was teaching in the temple; and at night he went out, and abode in the mount that is called the mount of Olives" (Luke 21:37). I suspect the Lord, in His private hours after the daytime work was done, was pleading with the Father to know what the Father would have Him do next.

Joy. Along with having the most glorious message available in the world, your purpose, along with all Heavenly Father's children, is to have joy (see 2 Nephi 2:25). That joy needs to be reflected in your face, in your demeanor, in your handshake, in the words you use. Your outward joy comes from the inner love you carry for those you meet.

Allow me to relate a personal story of a leader—a most effective teacher—who exemplified joy. In the April 2019 general conference, Elder Quentin L. Cook shared the following:

> I was exposed to the relationship between missionary work and love early in my life. When I was 11 years old, I received a patriarchal blessing from a patriarch who was also my grandfather. That blessing said in part, "I bless you with great love for your fellowmen, for thou shalt be called to carry the gospel to the world . . . to win souls unto Christ."
>
> I understood even at that early age that sharing the gospel was based on a great love for all our Heavenly Father's children. . . .
>
> When members gain a vision of this kind of love, which is essential in assisting the Lord in His purpose, the Lord's work will be accomplished. ("Great Love for Our Father's Children," *Ensign*, May 2019)

Years before this address was given, I was invited to visit with Elder Cook about the subject of missionary work. Having never been "summoned" to meet with a General Authority in the Church Office Building, I was part excited, part petrified. But as I walked down the hall to his office, I will never forget the wide, radiant smile on Elder Cook's face. He was literally standing in the hall outside his office, arms at his side, waiting to welcome me and my associate, Tom Peterson. He instantly put us at ease with his warmth and firm handshake. I was led to feel that a discussion with me was something he truly had been looking forward to. Imagine that!

Elder Cook has been blessed with an ability to love God's children, and it shows. He doesn't hide or suppress it. He uses this gift to further the work of the Lord. And I'm better because of it.

If you don't have a natural tendency to smile, pray that it might become a part of you as it is of Elder Cook. Emulate our Apostle. Let all the people you meet know that it is a joy to serve and teach them.

Appropriate humor. If you're living with joy, you'll find that humor will sometimes slip in, and it should—if it's appropriate. You don't have to be a stand-up comic to know that humor is a gift that can change the mood of a room and can lighten the burdens and concerns people bear.

If you're not convinced that humor is a powerful teaching tool, listen to some of the talks given by President Gordon B. Hinckley. With his gift for wit, he brought perspective and achieved great influence. In a particularly warm afternoon session of the October 1993 general conference in the Salt Lake Tabernacle and in between speakers, President Hinckley stood and said to those gathered, "We know it's warm in here. We're sorry. You're not nearly as warm as you will be if you don't repent."

***

As you reflect on the most successful missionaries you know, you'll recognize many other attributes—attributes you would do well to adopt. Those missionaries are likely knowledgeable, credible (they walk the talk), focused, flexible (able to switch topics when needed), encouraging, interesting, and engaging. Caution: while missionaries are "instruments in the hands of God" (Mosiah 17:36), you are not there to perform or show off talents. Your duty is to bring glory to God, never yourself, through the abilities He gifts to you.

If you want to be an effective teacher—missionary—watch others who are and do what they do. You can pray for these attributes but remember what the Lord told Oliver Cowdery: you must do more than just ask (see D&C 9:7). Think things through, seek or request some skills training if you need it, practice the attributes and skills you want to attain, and then ask the Lord to grant your righteous desire. He wants you to be the best you can be in teaching His gospel—and He *will* help.

Find someone in the mission you admire, who you think is an outstanding teacher, who you think is an outstanding companion, who always seems to show love unfeigned, who accepts transfers with patience, who demonstrates humility, and who works with enthusiasm. Find a missionary who possesses any one or all of these traits, and then work to emulate that missionary.

Of course, the Savior is always our ultimate role model. But the missionary you choose to emulate is *doing* what the Savior would do. It's no accident that those kinds of missionaries are successful. To know Him is to be like Him.

Principle 3: Don't Distract from the Spirit

Ready for this?

"Nothing you do as a missionary should get in the way of your important message: not your dress, not your hair length, your attitude; not your deportment; and not your girlfriend at home" (James E. Faust, "What I Want My Son to Know Before He Leaves On His Mission," *Ensign*, May 1996). President Faust didn't pull any punches. (And sisters, if his address hadn't been in a priesthood session of general conference, I think he would have said something very similar to you.)

The third principle in becoming an effective teacher and missionary is to make sure you don't distract from the Spirit of the Lord. To prevent that from ever happening, you need to understand what's called the "principle of distraction."

President Dallin H. Oaks taught this principle in a priesthood training session I attended many years ago in my home stake. It has stayed with me ever since, and it has helped me in my attempts to become a better teacher of the gospel.

Here's how I would describe it.

Imagine that you're entering the chapel for sacrament meeting. There are greeters at each of the two doors.

One greeter is a very disheveled young man. He's got a bad case of bed head—in fact, it appears his hair hasn't encountered a mirror in six weeks. Partly untucked, his shirt is so wrinkled it looks like he took it out of his backpack. The collar is unbuttoned, and the tie knot is drooping halfway down his chest. His hands are shoved in his pockets, and he's staring at the floor as he leans against the wall. He resembles a human question mark.

Okay. Quite a sight.

Now, we've all been taught not to judge. But realistically speaking, we do it every day. You see, making a judgment is different than judging a person. Judging is not our right, but making a judgment is how we protect ourselves. *I don't think I should go down that dark alley*, or *I should avoid that discussion they're having.* Neither of these involve taking bets on someone's salvation; they're just examples of someone making a judgment to avoid potential harm.

So, what are your first thoughts when seeing this "greeter"? You might think he's lazy or bored. You might guess that he's not very happy to be at church. You might speculate that he's rather disinterested. And you'll likely suppose that he's disconnected from what is happening—or should be happening—in this chapel. And, face it—he's no greeter.

Now imagine that this is the first time you've ever been to a sacrament meeting, and your first contact is this young man. What might you think of the church he represents? Based on his appearance and demeanor, you might conclude that it's boring, or that it doesn't teach much about happiness, or that it's a waste of people's time.

Your first impression of the greeter can cause you to cast judgment on the rest of the church. It's human nature to judge based on first impressions. And even though you could be *way* off in your assumptions, you'll probably make a negative judgment about this church, about its teachings, and about the people inside the chapel—all based on the appearance of one person. (Please note: we're not talking about judging people, we're talking about judgments that are made based on people.)

Now consider the greeter at the door on the other side of the chapel, a young woman about the same age as the disheveled greeter on the opposite side. She's standing up straight. She's obviously spent some time on her appearance. Her clothes are clean and pressed. She has a smile on her face. She is greeting each person with a warm hand-shake and a sincere welcome. If there's a visitor, she introduces herself by name and asks the visitor's name.

What kind of message is this greeter conveying? She's probably happy. She seems glad to be at church. She likely values and enjoys the kinds of things she learns in sacrament meeting. She probably has lots of friends here.

Just by looking at her, you get a completely different perspective on the Church. That's because she embodies all the great things about it. She demonstrates that the Church is a place of fellowship. It's a place where Saints gather. Looking at her demeanor, you decide this is the type of community you want to be part of—and if you're a parent, the kind of environment you want your kids to be in. All a result of her appearance and manner.

Preach My Gospel advises that you remove distractions "so that the Spirit of the Lord will not be hindered" (*Preach My Gospel*, 176). Here's a sobering thought: sometimes you and I, as faithful members of the Church, may look, dress, or behave in a way that is a distraction. Despite your good intentions, you might actually "hinder" the presence of the Spirit.

That's what President Oaks taught at our priesthood training session. He said to be careful about how you are at church—and for you as a missionary, that applies to everywhere you go. Be careful about how you dress. About how you speak. About your very manner. Because if you're not careful, he taught us, the distractions you cause will detract from the Spirit. And if you hinder the Spirit, you are preventing another person from feeling that influence or from focusing on the things they *should* be as they attend their church meetings, partake in the sacramental ordinance, or listen to you and others teach.

Think about sacrament meeting. When a deacon passes the sacrament to me and my wife, I hope he is clean and dressed in appropriate clothes. I don't want him to dress or act in a way that will distract from that sacred ordinance. You might say it's *my* problem if I get distracted. But I probably wouldn't have been distracted otherwise. It's the same reason we ask Church members to dress modestly. People may think an immodest article of clothing is fine, but if it contributes to others not having a clear mind to focus on the Spirit, it becomes a hindrance *to* the Spirit. What a shame if a minister of the Lord is the cause of such an impediment.

Now that you've trained your mind's eye on the greeters at the chapel door and the deacon who's passing the sacrament, you've probably figured out a whole new reason why Church leaders ask missionaries to dress modestly and purposefully. It's because missionaries are ambassadors for the Savior—and dressing the part helps you look and act like it.

When you show up on the doorstep dressed appropriately, you gain immediate credibility. You're taken seriously because you're dressed seriously. What do you think would happen if you were decked out in shorts, a t-shirt, and flip-flops—or how about a mini-skirt or cropped top for the sisters?

Your appearance is critical. But as a missionary, even as an ordained servant of the Lord, there are lots of *other* ways you can distract from the Spirit. As your companion teaches, you might be busy playing with the cat. Or you might be thumbing through some pamphlets or diving into your bag. While you're teaching, you might be chewing gum. Or drumming your fingers or tapping your foot. And regardless of which of you is teaching, your investigator will be spending more time counting the movie characters on the tie Aunt Karen sent you or wondering how you got the tear in your dress than concentrating on the scriptures you're sharing.

Don't be a distraction. Look at your companion and your investigator. Give both your undivided attention. Actively affirm what each is saying by the expression on your face or a subtle nod of your head.

Emulate Alma the Younger, a wonderful teaching companion. He sat quietly—and I'm sure attentively—as Amulek powerfully taught the contentious Zeezrom. Instead of interrupting his companion, Alma, recognizing that Amulek was filled with the Spirit, let him teach.

Then, "Alma . . . opened his mouth and began to speak unto him and to *establish the words of Amulek*, and to explain things beyond, or to unfold the scriptures beyond that which Amulek had done" (Alma 12:1; emphasis added). Alma felt no need to "get a word in." He humbly witnessed his companion filled with the Spirit, and he did not distract. In fact, by "establishing the words of Amulek," he acted as a second witness to his companion by pointing out the truthfulness of what he had taught (see also Alma 12:12, 24).

At the risk of sounding parental, go to bed on time so you can pay attention to what your companion is teaching and how your investigator is responding. Care for your health so you can be at the top of your game.

Please, never distract from the Spirit. The message you're delivering, and the Person for whom you are sharing it, is too important. And the brief time you spend with an investigator may be his or her only chance to feel that Witness.

Principle 4: Proclaim the Gospel with Urgency

Early in Christ's ministry, as He was performing miracles and preaching to all who would hear, His disciples became concerned that perhaps He was working too hard—over-extending Himself:

Therefore said the disciples one to another, hath any man brought him ought to eat?

Jesus saith unto them, My meat is to do the will of him that sent me, and to finish his work.

Say not ye, There are yet four months, and then cometh harvest? Behold, I say unto you, *Lift up your eyes, and look on the fields; for they are white already to harvest.* (John 4:33–35; emphasis added)

More than two thousand years ago—before the gathering of Israel began in earnest—Jesus Christ had a sense of urgency in His work. Or, more accurately, in the work of His Father. Just think how much more urgent the work is today in this, the *last* dispensation of the fulness of times!

"Our concern for our brothers and sisters," explains Elder Neil L. Andersen, "and our desire to please God bring a compelling urgency to share and strengthen the kingdom of God across the world" ("A Witness of God," *Ensign*, November 2016).

As a set apart servant of the Lord, there's no time to be casual about your message. Yours is a voice of warning, not passiveness. Warning voices have a sense of urgency.

You'll find that admonition in the scriptures. Doctrine and Covenants 112 is a section given to Thomas B. Marsh, who for a time was President of the Quorum of the Twelve Apostles. He'd had a problem with pride, which led him to lose favor with the Lord for a while. But he repented. And the Lord accepted his repentance.

Look at what the Lord then asked Brother Marsh to do: "Contend thou, therefore, morning by morning; and day after day let thy warning voice go forth; and when the night cometh let not the inhabitants of the earth slumber, because of thy speech" (D&C 112:5).

The Lord taught Brother Marsh the urgency necessary to share the gospel. He was told never to let up on proclaiming it. He was told to focus on it day by day, night by night. In fact, it seems the Lord was telling Brother Marsh, "As part of your repentance process, you need to proclaim the gospel with more urgency."

What about that seemingly strange instruction to "let not the inhabitants of the earth slumber, because of thy speech"? Does that mean you're supposed to stand outside the window and shout your message at all hours, keeping neighbors and investigators awake all night? No. It means that the gospel you're teaching is keeping them up at night because it's working inside of them. The Spirit they felt—the one you identified for them—is making them want to act on what they learn. That means you are not only proclaiming the gospel with urgency, but you *create* urgency in those who listen.

Let's look at some missionaries who felt and acted on urgency. When Jesus called His twelve disciples—the first missionaries in His time—at least four of them were busy fishing. Look what happened:

> And Jesus, walking by the sea of Galilee, saw two brethren, Simon called Peter, and Andrew his brother, casting a net into the sea: for they were fishers.
>
> And he saith unto them, Follow me, and I will make you fishers of men.
>
> And they straightway left their nets, and followed him.
>
> And going on from thence, he saw other two brethren, James the son of Zebedee, and John his brother, in a ship with Zebedee their father, mending their nets; and he called them.
>
> And they immediately left the ship and their father, and followed him. (Matthew 4:18–22)

Read that again. They didn't say, "Jesus, hang on. I've got a big one on the line!"

They didn't say, "Why did you call us *now?* We're breaking records with this haul. Have you seen the price of fish in the market? I'm makin' a killing this year!"

No. They felt the urgency of proclaiming the gospel message. They laid down their nets and "straightway"—in other words, *immediately*—followed Him.

These obedient followers didn't let anything else get in the way—not even their livelihood. Your choice to serve a mission today is the same choice those fishermen made two millennia ago. But the need for urgent action has only increased. In this dispensation, the Lord said, "Behold, I will hasten my work in its time" (D&C 88:73).

What does *urgency* look like? To answer that question, consider that God is urgently warning us about all kinds of things. He does it through His prophets. And He doesn't shout. In fact, He speaks with a still, small voice that, though it's a whisper, pierces all things (see D&C 85:6). And only those who are prepared will hear.

Urgency is *not* getting people to do something they don't want to do. That's not urgency. That's deception. That's manipulation. It's force. You never want to manipulate or coerce someone into the waters of baptism.

Urgency is helping someone obtain what they want or need today instead of waiting until tomorrow. You know what the scriptures say: don't procrastinate (put off until tomorrow) what you can do today (see Alma 34:33). In other words, why put off the results the gospel brings?

There are lots of things your investigators might want to do. They might want to repent and feel the relief that comes with it. They might want to stop smoking. They might want to stop verbally abusing a family member. There might be other things they need to put behind them.

There are also things they need to do. They need to start paying tithing. They need to keep the Sabbath day holy. They need to attend sacrament meeting and partake of the sacrament. Where does urgency fit in to all that? When you proclaim with urgency, you help people understand that by taking action *now*, they will get more of the results they're looking for *sooner.*

There's that word again: *results.* And here's where agency dovetails nicely with results. Once you identify which results are most important to an investigator, you can say, "You could get that result this afternoon. Would that be better than getting it next week?" Well of course! Who *wants* to put off to another day something they desire now?

Elder Dieter F. Uchtdorf put it this way:

To those who have not yet begun, why delay? If you want to experience the wonders of this great spiritual journey, set foot upon your own grand adventure! Speak with the missionaries. Speak with your Latter-day Saint friends. Speak with them about this marvelous work and a wonder. It's time to begin! ("Your Great Adventure," *Ensign*, November 2019)!

Why put off results until tomorrow when you can relish them today?

I'm not trying to suggest that someone should step into the baptismal font this afternoon. I will stress, though, that results can start to appear immediately in small, simple ways.

For example, an investigator could get certain immediate results by committing today to no longer use foul language. A father could get certain results today simply by saying *I love you* to his son when he leaves for school in the morning—something the father may not be accustomed to doing. A mother could get a result today by attending church with her member friend or with the missionaries. And she doesn't have to be a member of the Church to get those results. You can tell her with confidence, "Just by participating in our worship service this morning, I testify that you and your family will have greater peace in your home this afternoon!"

Make sure those you teach understand this principle. Make sure they know the results and the rewards can come immediately. The blessings don't just appear on that special date of baptism.

The awesome part of it is this: taking action in response to your urgency doesn't mean people have to eat the whole elephant in one sitting. They can do it a single bite at a time, and they'll still get results.

That's where encouragement comes in. Yes, investigators need to know that baptism is an outward sign of one's loyalty to the Savior. But they also need to know that as they work *toward* baptism, they can take lots of smaller steps that will bring them greater happiness, prosperity, peace, assurance, love. Those small steps might be a warm feeling in their heart. It might be a greater relationship with their spouse, who is touched by their new efforts.

There are so many results that could come from taking a small action in obedience to the gospel of Jesus Christ. That's the purpose and promise of the small commitments you ask investigators to make every time you visit with them.

Let them know that these small commitments—like reading a chapter of the Book of Mormon before your next visit—will bring positive results. Share with them what the result might be. And what if you're not sure which result they could see? Ask them what they'd like to get by accomplishing that task, then pray with them that Heavenly Father might grant it.

Just as your investigators need to know that they will get results from action, they also need to know that there are consequences to inaction. "And another also said, Lord, I will follow thee; but let me first go bid them farewell, which are at home at my house. And Jesus said unto him, No man, having put his hand to the plough, and looking back, is fit for the kingdom of God" (Luke 9:61–62). If God is ready to bless them, delaying righteous action offends Him and may disqualify that person from the very blessings Father is ready to push "send" on.

Gently, lovingly, but with the mantle of someone who has been sent to warn, you need to share possible consequences of inaction. After all, as a set apart minister, you're qualified and have the authority to do that. Help people understand that through inaction, they lose the potential of certain results—like having more love in their home or having greater closeness to their Father in Heaven.

Did you ever stop to think that you're an expert in consequences? You see good ones and bad ones *every day* in people who do or do not choose to live the gospel. That's part of urgency—speak with boldness in sharing your observations and counseling when asked. Relate the special things you've seen when others have responded and taken immediate action.

If when communicating these observations you feel too forward—even pushy—perhaps you can begin by saying, "Brother Gordon, we're not trying to be pushy, we're simply trying to be helpful. Allow us to share an example of another person we've been teaching. . . ."

To your investigator: why put off happiness? Why put off contentment? Why put off peace? Why put off success in the family, and prosperity in all that you do? Pray for help in teaching your investigator the results of acting on a gospel principle today.

And, dear missionaries, the same thing applies to you. Maybe you'll need to apply repentance to your life. Maybe you won't treat a companion very well. Maybe you won't work as hard as you should in an area. Maybe you murmur a little bit (or a lot) about a policy the mission president and his wife establish. Don't worry about being right, just strive to be more righteous. Use repentance.

President Nelson warned and encouraged us when he said, "When we choose to repent, we choose to change! We allow the Savior to transform us into the best version of ourselves." Why would anyone want to put that off?

He continued, especially for those involved in missionary work: "Daily repentance is the pathway to purity, and purity brings power. Personal purity can make us powerful tools in the hands of God. Our repentance—our purity—will empower us to help in the gathering of Israel" ("We Can Do Better and Be Better," *Ensign*, May 2019).

Though his counsel came decades ago, there is much to learn from this apostolic counsel on urgency given by Elder Neal A. Maxwell in general conference:

> I should like to speak of and to a particular group of important individuals. These are they who fully intend, someday, to begin to believe and/or to be active in the Church. But not yet! These are not bad individuals, but good individuals who simply do not know how much better they could be. . . . These are they who need and are needed by the Church, but who, in part, "live without God in the world." . . .
>
> There are reasons for your commitments to be made now, for as the rush of hours, days, and months grows stronger, the will to commit grows weaker. . . .
>
> Act, my brothers and sisters, for once the soul is tilted toward belief, and once there is even a desire to believe, then

marvelous things begin to happen! ("Why Not Now?" *Ensign*, November 1974)

Do you see what he's saying? Marvelous *results* begin to happen the moment they decide!

Elder Maxwell reminded us that Joshua told us to choose "this day" who we would serve. Joshua didn't tell you to "choose this year" or to "choose sometime between now and next summer." No. He said, "choose you *this day* whom ye will serve" (Joshua 24:15; emphasis added). *That* is urgency.

Noah did not wait until it started raining to build the ark. As soon as he received instruction, "Noah did according to all that the Lord commanded him" (Genesis 7:5). The sky might have been cloudless, but Noah acted anyway. *That* is urgency.

More than twenty-five years after I left my full-time service in Japan, Elder Kazuhiko Yamashita of the Seventy urged missionaries of the Church in general conference: "People all over the world are waiting for you. Please go quickly to where they are. No one strives harder than missionaries to go to the rescue of others. I am one of those rescued" ("Missionaries Are a Treasure of the Church," *Ensign*, November 2011).

Now it's up to you to proclaim the message with urgency—not to grow your numbers, and not to impress the mission office with your statistics—but to more quickly bring to people's lives the results and blessings the Lord is waiting to pour down upon them.

Chapter Four

Your Voice Is Your Suit

(Sisters, This Is for You Too)

"Yea, Lord, thy watchmen shall lift up their voice."

Abinadi, quoting Isaiah, Mosiah 15:29

Here's something you've probably never considered: as a mission-ary, your voice is your suit.

What? I'm supposed to wear my voice?

Kind of. Because just as your attire says what kind of person you are and conveys your attitude about what you're doing (remember those greeters in Chapter Three?), so does your voice.

You'll find that sometimes your voice is your only physical tool. If you're on the phone—in the MTC Referral Center, in the mission office, or setting up a first-time appointment with an investigator—it won't matter that you're wearing a Gucci suit. It won't matter that you're having the best hair day ever. It won't matter that you've got the trendiest shoes on the planet. Because whoever you're talking to can't see any of that. All they can hear is your voice.

So your voice matters—a *lot*—even when you're looking at some-one face to face.

Think about this. What if you introduce yourself and the gospel message with a flat, monotone voice? What does that say about you? About the gospel? It says the same thing as that disheveled greeter at the chapel door: You're disinterested. Bored. Tired. Perhaps worst of all, it suggests you *expect* rejection.

Whether you're sitting in their family room or on the phone, think about what your monotone voice is *saying*: "Hey, I'm calling [or I'm here] because uh . . . we know one of your friends, and, uh, they gave us your name and said you might want a Book of Mormon. No? Yeah, I didn't really think so. Okay. Sorry to bother you."

Wait! You'd never actually say those words! (Of course, you wouldn't.) But guess what? That's *exactly* what your voice might convey. Your voice might sound like it's wearing a pressed suit, or it might sound like it's got on old gym shorts, a stained t-shirt, and some battered flip-flops.

As a missionary, your message is the good news. It's the most important message on earth. You don't control the content of your message—it's in the scriptures and throughout Church manuals and delivered over the pulpit in general conference. But you *do* control the way you deliver that message. Does your voice belittle the "word"? Does your voice help or hinder that which you're called to proclaim?

Just from the way you sound, regardless of how you look, you gain or lose credibility and trust. Maybe a member wants to give you a referral—are you going to treat that referral carefully, with respect and dignity? Or are you going to embarrass the person who gave you the referral?

Your voice might cause the member to think, *You know what? I'm not going to entrust my friends, my relatives, or my nonmember mother to you because I don't trust that you're really going to take it seriously. There's very little energy or sincerity when you talk, and this person is way too important for me to share their name with just anybody. Maybe I'll just wait for the next missionary.*

Believe me on this: most people will make a judgment about you and your message based on your voice—how you communicate and how you speak. Do you sound tired and worn out, like you want to go back to the apartment—or anywhere but here? Is the only time they hear excitement in your voice when you talk about your high school playing days or your hobby back home? Or does your voice communicate energy and enthusiasm, your belief that this just might be the best day of your mission?

If you want to be successful as a missionary, act successful. That means you need to *sound* successful. Sound like you're already successful, and you soon will be. Because that's the only kind of person people want to talk to, give referrals to, invite in their home, be taught by. They don't want to talk to someone who sounds dejected; they want to associate with someone who is enthused about their message—even if it's not being well-received on this particular day—because that message is so hopeful and joyful. Think about it this way: your voice should sound like it's *smiling*.

With a little effort, you can do it.

"Use Boldness, Not Overbearance"

Our Church leaders—our effective, experienced teachers—"use boldness, but not overbearance" (Alma 38:12). It is manifested in two ways: what they say, and how they say it.

I'll leave the "what" to the Brethren and general officers of the Church, but let's take a closer look at the "how."

I'll never forget the firm yet gentle voice Elder Jeffrey R. Holland used to chastise, then encourage, the Church membership in his landmark April 2019 general conference talk, "Behold, the Lamb of God" (*Ensign*, May 2019). It's a wonderful example of how a voice that is at one time stern and in another instant soothing can effectively captivate and teach the word of God.

In that same conference, Elder Quentin L. Cook shared a story of how Otto Haleck, a respected citizen in Samoa, was the patriarch of a large family of Latter-day Saints, though Otto himself had never joined the Church. Playing host to many visiting General Authorities, including Elder Cook while he served as president of the Pacific Isles Area, Otto resisted all attempts to be taught the gospel. He resisted, that is, until President Gordon B. Hinckley lodged at his home for the Suva Fiji Temple dedication.

Elder Cook recounts:

When we gathered for breakfast the next morning, President Hinckley and Otto Haleck had already become good friends. It was interesting to me that they were having much the same conversation I had had with Otto more than a year earlier. When Otto expressed his admiration for our Church but reaffirmed his commitment to his existing church, President Hinckley put his hand on Otto's shoulder and said, "Otto, that's not good enough; you ought to be a member of the Church. This is the Lord's Church." You figuratively could see the resistive armor fall away from Otto with an openness to what President Hinckley said.

This was the beginning of additional missionary teaching and a spiritual humility that allowed Otto Haleck to be baptized and confirmed a little over a year later. One year after that, the Haleck family was sealed as an eternal family in the temple. ("Great Love for Our Father's Children," *Ensign*, May 2019)

The Lord's missionaries are bold, but not overbearing. Notice how before he could express boldness ("Otto, that's not good enough"), President Hinckley became Otto Haleck's friend.

President Russell M. Nelson shared the following:

Many years ago, two colleagues of mine—a nurse and her doctor husband—asked me why I lived the way I did. I answered, "Because I know the Book of Mormon is true." I let them borrow my copy of the book, inviting them to read it. A week later they returned my book with a polite "thanks a lot."

I responded, "What do you mean, thanks a lot? That's a totally inappropriate response for one who has read this book. You didn't read it, did you! Please take it back and read it; then I would like my book back."

Admitting that they had only turned its pages, they accepted my invitation. When they returned, they said tearfully, "We have read the Book of Mormon. We know it is true! We want to know more." They learned more, and it was my privilege to baptize both of them. ("Be Thou an Example of the Believers," *Ensign*, November 2010)

Ordained ministers are not afraid to be bold (see Ephesians 6:19–20). They know that if they speak the words of Christ and invite with love, the Spirit can soften the hearts of the hearer, and the truth their friend knew premortally will suddenly sound familiar.

Despite the eventual wickedness of Laman and Lemuel, there was a time after Nephi received the interpretation of his father's dream of the tree of life that he, Nephi, "did speak many words unto my brethren, that they were pacified and did humble themselves before the Lord. . . . I did exhort them with all the energies of my soul, and with all the faculty which I possessed" (1 Nephi 15:20, 25).

Watch how the General Authorities and your mission president teach. Notice how they sometimes whisper, sometimes speak loudly, and commonly vary their voice to carry their message. This is not to manipulate or entertain. It is to distinctly communicate their testimony and the surety of it.

Six Tools of the Spirit

The first account we have of the Holy Ghost testifying in the ancient days is when two disciples were on the way to Emmaus following Christ's resurrection. "And they said one to another, Did not our heart burn within us, while he *talked* with us. . . ?" (Luke 24:32; emphasis added). The Spirit testifies when truthful words are spoken. We sometimes feel the same when we hear others bear a testimony.

If missionaries, then, use words to witness of the truthfulness of the gospel of Jesus Christ, and if your voice is the instrument by which these words are delivered, then it stands to reason that the Spirit can bless your voice to carry out this work.

Here are six ways your voice may help you become a more compelling teacher. Between you and your companion, use these six tools in every encounter, whether you're teaching a lesson, meeting someone on the street, or following up with a phone call.

Turn Up the Volume

What happens to a class when a teacher suddenly gets LOUD? That's right: they wake up. If they've been sleepy or daydreaming or distracted or thinking about anything else besides what's going on in class, that ramp-up in volume gets their attention. Right away.

To be clear, I'm not suggesting you should start shouting at some poor investigator. Nor should you deliver your message in an ear-splitting tone. But sometimes temporarily boosting the volume at an appropriate time can cause people to be more tuned in to what you're saying.

In Lehi's dream of the tree of life, he used volume to make sure his family knew the urgency with which he wanted them to join him: "I also did say unto them with a loud voice that they should come . . . partake of the fruit" (1 Nephi 8:15).

Whisper

On the other hand, what happens when a teacher suddenly lapses into an intense whisper? You know—the kind that creates interest, not the kind no one can hear. It pulls the class in. They lean forward. They get very focused on what's being said.

You can effectively use a whisper—just remember that a whisper doesn't mean low energy. It means low *volume*. Don't use a whisper that nobody can reasonably hear; just lower your voice enough to garner greater attention.

Speak Swiftly

Sometimes very effective teachers get talking really fast about a certain topic. You've probably heard that happen. Speaking-rapidly-creates-a-sense-of-excitement! It heightens the energy in the room. Listeners can't help but look up. They want to see what's going on—to be a part of it.

Again, moderation is the key. Don't deliver an entire lesson with reckless speed. Just know when to step it up to stress an important point.

Speak Slowly

At the opposite end of the spectrum, slow down when . . . there's . . . something . . . you . . . really . . . want . . . to . . . emphasize. You need your investigator to really pay attention. You don't want him to miss a syllable. Whether you do it in a soft or a loud voice, it says, "Pay attention to what we're saying right now."

Repeat Yourself

Sometimes it's effective to repeat a point you just made. Why? Because by repeating it you highlight that point. You focus attention on that principle. You call attention to that scripture. You underscore a challenge. Again, you highlight that point. You focus attention on that principle. You call attention to that scripture. You underscore a challenge. (See what I did there?)

Use Emphasis

When you emphasize a *certain* word or phrase, you're telling your investigator to listen carefully. You're saying it's the most important principle you're going to teach that day, and you don't want them to miss a *single* word.

A Bonus: Practice!

You were not called on a mission to write the gospel. Unless, like one of my sons, you were blessed enough to receive an assignment to work among the deaf, you were called to *preach* the gospel using your mouth and your voice. So you need to exercise this important tool you've been given to do God's work.

Here's what it boils down to: practice. You're like a gifted athlete. Do you think professional athletes just lounge on the bench and say, "Hey, coach, I'm just gonna hang out here until warm-ups are over. Lemme know when the game starts"? Not a chance! Serious athletes stretch out and warm up before a game; they loosen up and break a sweat. And when they're not playing, they're practicing.

Just like that athlete, *you* need to break a missionary sweat in your apartment before you leave to start teaching that day. How can the Lord fill your mouth with words if you won't open it (see D&C 33:8, 71:1)? Wouldn't it be easier for the Lord to loosen your tongue (D&C 11:21) when you have done your part to physically prepare for it?

Here's how: Start your day by reading out loud. When you read your scriptures in the morning, read a portion of them out loud with your companion and by yourself. Practice opening your mouth. Literally. Stretch your lips and tongue.

I know you think that's silly, but the first time you try to become expressive each day should not be in front of an investigator. Instead, it should be a warm-up exercise in your personal or companion study. Don't be shy; you weren't called on a mission to give in to your inhibitions, but to speak up, with boldness. As companions, be understanding and encouraging and cut each other some slack. No making fun!

If you'll start with this exercise, practicing the six tools of the Spirit you just learned, you can speak with confidence as soon as you step out of your apartment. You never want to sound as if you just woke up. You want to make it sound like you have been awake for hours; your voice then says, "I love this message, and I'm excited to share it with everyone!"

And there's another great way to exercise and practice: Teach your companion. I'm serious. Practice the six tools as you teach. Do part of it in a loud voice. Recite a quote in a very intense whisper. Repeat the key phrases in a verse of scripture. And try emphasizing words that don't even deserve it, just to see how it works. Ask yourself as you practice, *Is this the way the prophet would present this lesson? Is this the kind of energy Alma might use to present this doctrine?* Remember, your goal is to learn from the best.

This is not as weird as it might sound. Most of your "fellow missionaries" who speak in general conference invest time preparing to teach with the right voice. It's one of the best things you can do to avoid being misunderstood or misjudged—and one of the best ways you can ensure that your message is properly delivered.

Open Your Mouth

You may feel inhibited and shy about opening your mouth. You're not alone. But know that the Lord has a mission even for the slow of speech. Upon receiving his mission call, Moses said, "O my Lord, I am not eloquent . . . but I am slow of speech, and of a slow tongue" (Exodus 4:10).

Similarly, Enoch protested that God had chosen the wrong servant when he said, "Why is it that I have found favor in thy sight, and am but a lad, and all the people hate me; for I am slow of speech; wherefore [why] am I thy servant?" (Moses 6:31).

Take into your own heart what the Lord answered Enoch: "Go forth and do as I have commanded thee, and no man shall pierce thee. Open thy mouth, and it shall be filled, and I will give thee utterance, for all flesh is in my hands, and I will do as seemeth me good" (Moses 6:32).

The Lord, speaking of a group of elders who were standing around wondering what to do next, told the Prophet Joseph Smith, "But with some I am not well pleased, for they will not open their mouths, but they hide the talent which I have given unto them, because of the fear of man. Wo unto such, for mine anger is kindled against them" (D&C 60:2).

Yikes.

I don't know about *you*, but the last thing I'd want as one of His ordained ministers is for the Lord's anger to be kindled against me.

Missionaries need to open their mouths. Literally. They need to try to speak like the angels speak, even like the great prophets of the Book of Mormon spoke. Abinadi wasn't reserved in his speech. He spoke with such power that he terrified the unrighteous people who heard him (see Mosiah 13:5). Even in the waning moments of his life, he spoke with great power (see Mosiah 17:9–20).

I get it. You're *not* Abinadi, and public speaking—even one-on-one conversations—can be scary. On top of that, you might be faced with speaking to someone twice your age. Someone who is the CEO of a major corporation. Someone who is a political leader. Or maybe a minister of another church. Under such a circumstance, you might think, *I don't have their experience, their presence, their clout.*

Never forget: you have something they don't have. You have the promise of a Savior who has told you that if you lift up your voice and speak what He puts into your heart, you *will not be confounded* before men. In fact, He will give you in the very hour—the very *moment*—what you should say (see D&C 100:5–6).

In conclusion, and to prove what value opening your mouth will have on the gathering of Israel, let me share a story President Thomas S. Monson related of two missionaries serving in Canada. One snowy night while going from house to house, they were invited into the home of Mr. Elmer Pollard. Despite the fact that they presented a message, it was clear that their host was not capturing the spirit of it.

President Monson related:

> In due time he asked that they leave and not return. His last words to the elders as they departed his front porch were spoken in derision: "You can't tell me you actually believe Joseph Smith was a prophet of God!"
>
> The door was shut. The elders walked down the path. [The young missionary] spoke to his companion: "Elder, we didn't respond to Mr. Pollard. He said we didn't believe Joseph Smith was a true prophet. Let's return and bear our testimonies to him." At first the more experienced missionary hesitated but finally agreed to accompany his companion. Fear struck their hearts as they approached the door from which they had just been ejected. They knocked, confronted Mr. Pollard, spent an agonizing moment, and then with power borne of the Spirit, our inexperienced missionary spoke: "Mr. Pollard, you said we didn't really believe Joseph Smith was a prophet of God. I testify to you that Joseph *was* a prophet. He *did* translate the Book of Mormon. He saw God the Father and Jesus the Son. I know it."
>
> Some time later, Mr. Pollard, now Brother Pollard, stood in a priesthood meeting and declared, "That night I could not sleep. Resounding in my ears I heard the words 'Joseph Smith was a prophet of God. I know it. I know it. I know it.' The next

day I telephoned the missionaries and asked them to return. Their message, coupled with their testimonies, changed my life and the lives of my family." ("Come, All Ye Sons of God," *Ensign*, May 2013)

Now, go take care of that suit.

SECTION II

Seven Skills of a Successful Missionary

**"Remember that discipleship is not about doing
things perfectly; it's about doing things intentionally."**

Elder Dieter F. Uchtdorf,
"Your Great Adventure," *Ensign*, November 2019

In the last few chapters, we have explored many principles and practices that can lead to successfully preaching the gospel of Jesus Christ and gathering Israel. In the remaining chapters, we will take a deep dive into seven specific skills missionaries should acquire in order to "rise to a new sense of commitment to assist our Father in Heaven in His glorious work" (*Preach My Gospel*, v).

These skills cannot substitute for your personal study of the scriptures and Church-approved resources. But they are intended to further prepare you for the training you will obtain from *Preach My Gospel*, your mission president, mission training sessions, or instructions from Church leaders.

To become a successful missionary, here are the seven skills you'll need to develop:

1. Knowing how to build trust
2. Assessing for understanding
3. Presenting a tailored message
4. Proper listening to resolve concerns
5. Opening the gate to the covenant path

6.   Connecting through referrals
7.   Fellowshipping effectively

The order in which you apply these skills will depend on how your investigator responds (or doesn't respond). That response will be directly related to the investigator's background, history, interests, family situation, previous experience with the Church, and many other possible factors. What's important is not the order in which you use these skills, but that you master them so that the Spirit can rely on you and guide you in adapting them to your teaching needs.

As I teach these seven skills in the next seven chapters, I will use the word *investigator* to describe anyone with whom you interact who isn't already a member of The Church of Jesus Christ of Latter-day Saints, whether they be a street contact, a person at a door, or a fully engaged participant in your lessons. And for the sake of the seven skills we'll cover, let's imagine that you've got a willing investigator who, as part of their spiritual journey, moves with you through the whole process of accepting the gospel and receiving baptism.

Chapter Five

Skill 1: Knowing How to Build Trust

"Neglect not the gift that is in thee, which was given thee by prophecy, with the laying on of the hands. . . . Meditate upon these things; give thyself wholly to them; . . . for in doing this thou shalt both save thyself, and them that hear thee."

Apostle Paul, 1 Timothy 4:14–16

Hope you packed a lunch, because we're going to spend some significant time on this skill. Why? It's probably the most important skill a missionary—called by prophecy and set apart by the laying on of hands—can develop. Building relationships of trust will help you identify and focus on results important to anyone you meet within the *first fifteen seconds* of an encounter.

If investigators don't learn to trust you, they won't tell you what they need. They won't tell you what they want. They won't tell you what troubles them. They won't accept what you teach. And they'll never truly believe you or the message you teach. Which means, of course, your work as a missionary will be very short-lived.

As an ordained minister, you're asking investigators to trust you with a lot: their time, which nobody seems to have enough of; their energy, which some people lack; and their attention, which can easily get diverted. Eventually, you're asking them to trust you with their doubts and misgivings and reservations—because if you don't address those, investigators will never agree to make commitments.

And here's an even greater reason to build trust with your investigators. When you teach, you're acting on behalf of Jesus Christ—serving as a temporary, proxy savior, if you will. And if they come to trust you, His representative, you enable the investigator to learn to trust the Savior Himself.

This probably isn't a news flash to you, but there are a lot of things in this world that people *mistrust*. People have a healthy dose of skepticism about things on TV, radio, and the Internet—things that "invade" their homes and over which they have no sense of control. There's widespread mistrust of religion. There's mistrust of people who peddle things on the street and of people in general, especially young people. There's an increasing mistrust of anyone devoted to the clergy. Now look at yourself: people might see you as nothing more than a young, religious peddler. Building trust with the people you teach is a vital, yet tough, thing to do.

Let me share a personal story about my wife of thirty-three years, Allison, that says more than I ever could about trust between missionaries and an investigator. When we began dating in high school, I was anxious to introduce her to the missionaries at the appropriate time. Her family's standards were already exceptional, but I knew her life would be even more complete if she knew about the restored gospel. I was blessed to come from a missionary family where friends of my parents and siblings were often invited to meet with the missionaries. For me, it was just a natural thing to do.

Well, despite some protests from a couple of people close to Allison, she agreed to meet with me, my parents, and two missionaries at our home one night. Looking back, I realize it was five against one in that living room. Allison noticed it before I did.

The missionaries wasted no time and started out by challenging her to pray right there in front of us. She was very uncomfortable. That would be an appropriate request in some teaching environments *if* it came from distinct promptings. I can't say if it was or not. All I know is that Allison awkwardly resisted the request.

About half-way through the discussion, my best friend started crying. As a young man with limited experience in spiritual matters, I thought, *Oh, the Spirit is working. This is awesome! She's feeling it.*

But as the discussion ended and I walked her out to her car, she was still crying. Finally alone with me, she said, "That was the worst experience I've ever had. I was so embarrassed. Don't ask me to do that again!"

She got in her car and drove away.

I felt horrible. Not only did I fear our friendship may have just ended, but something I had anticipated for so long ended up being a miserable experience. Her tears weren't tears of joy—they were tears of humiliation. She was mortified about being put on the spot to pray and answer religious questions and share deep, personal thoughts she'd never before expressed. And she was expected to do it in the company of people she didn't know that well—including *two strangers.*

To my relief, we continued to be close friends. But you'd better believe we didn't talk about religion again for at least six months.

Over time, her heart softened, and I was humbled. My motives were cleansed, and I was better prepared to introduce her to the gospel in a way that didn't make her feel defensive.

Allison eventually engaged in the lessons with a different pair of missionaries. As you can imagine, in that first discussion she was very guarded. Cautious. And there was no mistake about it: I knew that if she had an experience with these missionaries like the previous one, our discussions about religion would be over.

As you can also imagine, I prayed. I prayed *hard* that the missionaries would be inspired to teach her the way she needed to be taught—that they'd use methods appropriate to her heart and her circumstances.

To my joy and relief, Allison did feel the Spirit in that second meeting with missionaries. Things went so well, in fact, that she opened up and agreed to join me as the two of us studied the scriptures together. Within a couple of months, she wanted to be baptized.

A month after graduation, and despite opposition, Allison was baptized a member of the Church. We eventually married and have raised a family together. She has been a wonderful mother, a marvelous grandmother, and an example to countless others. Had those second missionaries not been able to build trust with Allison, I can't imagine how different my life would be today.

***

Building trust with an investigator is a *process* that might take hours, days, weeks, or even longer. But there are things you can do in the first *fifteen seconds* of an encounter that will encourage investigators to give you a chance—to trust you with their time, energy, and attention.

The First Fifteen Seconds

The moment a new contact shows even a glimmer of interest, your tendency might be to immediately launch into a lesson or discussion. After all, that's what missionaries spend most of their time preparing for, right? But unless the Spirit gives you unmistakable direction to do that, I suggest you tap the brakes and slow down.

Think about it. You just met this person, and you don't know what's happened to him before this very minute. Maybe he doesn't trust people who go door-to-door (lots of people don't). Maybe organized religion scares him (it scares a lot of people). Maybe he's had a bad experience with a missionary before. Maybe he just doesn't like the way you comb your hair. Yet here you are, hoping to eventually discuss some very sensitive, personal, private things with him.

You need him to trust you.

"The first few moments with people are very important," teaches *Preach My Gospel*. "They must learn to trust you. Begin your first visit in a warm, respectful, genuine manner" (*Preach My Gospel*, 178).

Here's the beauty: that process can start within about fifteen seconds. *Fifteen seconds.*

If you do it right.

If you do it wrong, lots of things might flash through that investigator's mind. She might think you're pressured to hit a quota. She might think you're just trying to "get her" so you can increase church membership. She might even think you're out recruiting new converts to beef up a donation plate that's passed around on Sunday. And these are only a few of the possible misconceptions that might cause any investigator to mistrust you at first sight.

If you do it right, though, you'll say something in those first fifteen seconds that will pique the investigator's curiosity, that will build some interest, that will intrigue him or her to hear more. If you handle those first fifteen seconds the right way, they'll start to trust you—and invite you to tell them more. Maybe, eventually, a *lot* more.

How, then, should you begin a new interaction? You should deliver a *benefit statement*. It's a way of saying that a conversation with you is going to benefit that investigator. And that benefit statement takes about fifteen seconds.

The specific benefit statement you use will depend on the individual you're addressing. No two benefit statements will be exactly the same, because every person you approach is a little different. The Spirit will help you know what you need to say to that specific person. (This is another reason why you should constantly pray for the companionship and direction of the Spirit to know which *words* to use.)

To deliver an effective benefit statement in the first fifteen seconds to someone you've contacted on your own—not a referral, necessarily—do three things:

1. **Introduce yourself and your companion;**
2. **Say who or what you represent; and**
3. **Briefly explain the benefit that person will receive by talking with you.**

Those seem straightforward, right? But there are a few important things to keep in mind with all three.

First, the introduction. We're talking fifteen seconds, so don't go into the details—where you're from, how long you've been serving as a missionary, the history of your family. All of that can be shared later.

Remember, too, that at first you might be speaking different languages. I don't mean Finnish or French—I mean you could be using words and expressions the person doesn't understand. Our Latter-day Saint vocabulary is filled with terms and nuances that might baffle the average person. "Part of teaching for understanding is to make sure you explain words, phrases, and ideas so that other people understand you better" (*Preach My Gospel*, 184).

Keep that in mind, because you might have to quickly explain that all missionaries have the title *elder* or *sister*. (We've all heard it: "How funny that you both have the same first name!") In your fifteen seconds, you won't give all the background of *why* you're called *elder* or *sister*, but if necessary, you can specify that it's a title, *not* your first name.

And speaking of your name, *please say it slowly and clearly.* If people don't know each other's names, trust is always harder to obtain.

Second, who or what you represent. You should say, "I represent Jesus Christ" or "I'm a representative of The Church of Jesus Christ of Latter-day Saints." Speak clearly and succinctly—no mumbling. Say it with the honor and dignity and reverence it deserves.

Third, the benefit statement. Suggest the result the investigator will receive from your message. Choose something you think he'll want. As instructed in *Preach My Gospel*, "Help people see that [the message] will have personal relevance for them" (*Preach My Gospel*, 179). You probably won't know what his exact hot button is right now, so tap your experience talking to similar investigators. Use your intuition. By always relying on the Spirit, your "hunch" is more likely to reflect what the Lord would have you say. "You will be able to adjust your teaching as you listen to the promptings of the Spirit" (*Preach My Gospel*, 179).

Here's why a benefit statement is important. Consider the missionary who approaches the person on the street and right away says, "Aren't you glad to know there are modern-day prophets alive today?" Uh, no. People rarely head to work or to the store thinking,

I wonder if there are any modern-day prophets I don't know about? A question like that won't lead to conversation. It *will* lead to rejection. What works a lot better is to say something that very realistically could be on the person's mind.

Benefit statements are tailored to fit the situation—it will be different if you're in a crowded marketplace than if you're attending ward council for the first time. (Yes, benefit statements are useable with investigators *as well as* members. We'll get to that.)

Before we go further, a reminder: "It is essential to learn the [missionary lessons] but these should not be taught by rote presentation. The missionary should feel free to use his own words as prompted by the Spirit. He should not give a memorized recitation, but speak from the heart in his own terms" (*Preach My Gospel*, 177).

In that same spirit, I would recommend considering ahead of time some benefit statements that might work in certain situations, that can help you introduce yourself in the best light during those first fifteen seconds. You want to be comfortable, not comatose. Practicing would be wise. But don't memorize and then plan to toss out a rote statement.

Let's dive into some specifics.

Benefit Statements for Individual Investigators

You walk up to a house or apartment you've not visited before. You knock. Face it: whoever opens the door didn't expect to find two missionaries standing on the doorstep.

What now?

Be flexible. Your benefit statement won't be the same for everyone who answers the door.

Immediately consider the age of the person. If a young child answers, you don't need to worry about a benefit statement right up front—instead, you might ask, "Is your mommy or daddy home?" You want to find an adult (or at least a teenager) as quickly as possible. Otherwise, you might come under suspicion—and you don't need that.

If an elderly gentleman answers, on the other hand, your mind should immediately go to results a person in that age group could be interested in. And a woman in her forties will likely have different interests from a woman in her early twenties.

In addition to age, you should also consider gender—a benefit statement for a man may be different than one for a woman. Think about this, too: you can use certain words and phrases with a woman that would probably seem odd and awkward if used for a man, and vice versa.

The key is this: when organizing a benefit statement in your mind, consider who is in front of you and your first impression. You instantly recall the daily results (the exercise we did in Chapter One) that such a person is most likely trying to achieve or obtain through the gospel of Jesus Christ. Choose one or two, and speak.

It's smart to size up a person's demeanor or temperament the minute the door opens. If someone yanks open the door and abruptly asks, "What is it?" you'll need to use a different benefit statement than for someone who seems half asleep—or someone who seems excited to see you. (Believe it or not, that *does* occasionally happen.)

A good idea is to "mirror" the person at the door. An investigator will be more likely to talk to you if you possess a similar demeanor or temperament. If someone answers the door in a sour mood and barks, "What do you want?" you probably won't get far if you're enthusiastically popping your name tag off your shirt with, "Hi, there! We're representatives of The Church of Jesus Christ of Latter-day Saints, and we are so glad you're home!"

Changing your approach based on the situation you encounter isn't being insincere. It's being relatable. As long as you're not fake and you let your best personality radiate, it will increase the chance of establishing immediate rapport and trust with people you meet.

Sample Statements that Open Hearts and Minds—and Doors

I'm going to share here a few sample statements. These are just that: *samples*. It's up to you to put in the effort to improve them and personalize them to meet your circumstances. Fair warning: not everything will work in every situation—just ask the missionaries throughout the scriptures. But what I'll suggest should help increase the number of people who accept your effort and invite you to tell them more.

You might start out by saying, "We wanted to stop by today . . . " Consider what that says: "We're not visiting *every* house on your street today. We're visiting *your* home, because we want to share something with *you*."

You should also emphasize certain words or phrases, such as "to share a *brief thought*." That says you're not going to take up their entire day. Sure, you'd love to be invited inside—but the point of an initial contact is not to share every detail of the restored gospel at one time. You've probably caught someone in the middle of something—talking on the phone, fixing a faucet, eating dinner, or watching an exciting game. Respect that.

Now, a few sample results and the approach that might follow:

Result: personal peace or contentment. Since most people want peace, are seeking contentment, or are struggling with something that's causing pain, you can say something like:

"The reason we felt impressed to stop by your home today is to share with you a brief thought on how everyone can enjoy greater peace and happiness at home."

Who could dispute that? Honestly, will someone say, "That's the most ridiculous thing I've ever heard"? Okay, there are always exceptions. One or two cranky people might still toss you off the porch. Not likely, though.

Result: instilling values in children. Parents hope their kids will grow up to be good people. If you walk up a driveway and see a scooter, a glove, a ball and a bat scattered around the front porch, it's a good bet there's a family with children living in the home.

You might approach them with:

"We wanted to briefly stop by your home and invite you to hear a quick message that can help children make good choices when facing bad influences."

Most well-intentioned parents will not object to this benefit state-ment. They may later object to the Church, but you haven't said any-thing about that yet. All you're trying to do right now is build trust and share a message that's hard to reject.

And look at the way that statement is worded. You're *inviting*, not *telling*. Inviting someone is softer, gentler, and honors their agency. If you say instead, "We're going to give you a message," you're basically sticking your foot in the door and demanding they listen up. Not the friendliest way to approach people as a messenger for Christ.

There's another interesting thing in the way that statement is worded: when you talk about bad influences increasing around their children, you're showing the adult that you understand something about parenting. You're indicating that you can relate. You're demon-strating that you know something about their struggles, their hopes, their fears, their wishes. And you do it all in a fifteen-second approach that begins to build trust and rapport.

Result: enhancing family relationships. Maybe a husband and wife aren't getting along very well, and it's wrecking their day or their week or their life. They're constantly wracked with pain and frustration about their marriage. What result do they need? Family unity. (It's a commonly needed result among any set of people living in a shared space.) You might offer up:

"We're excited to share some encouraging suggestions that bring families together in a world that sometimes pulls us apart."

Examine the wording there, too. You're saying, "We're excited to share with you." You're not asking for donations. You're not asking them to come to church this Sunday. And you're not insisting they stop smoking right now. When you refer to "encouraging sugges-tions," you're letting them know that your message is one of hope and support. You're not there to criticize, because they get plenty of that in the world. You're there to help, encourage, and inspire. After all, isn't that what Jesus did?

Result: understanding the purpose of life's challenges. This is a pretty universal result, because everyone will at some time suffer or struggle over something. You have trials. Your zone leaders and mission president will have trials. Yes, your own family has trials. Trials are a part of life. Even though we all experience afflictions of some sort or another, everyone wants to better understand what their purpose in life is and how to make sense of those trials. Perhaps you could begin with:

"Our purpose for stopping by your home today is to bring a message of hope that helps people, regardless of their circumstances, better understand why we're here on earth and how we can overcome daily challenges."

When you say something like that, you're more likely to get the person's attention. People who hear it may think, *Wow, you understand. You may look like you're only twenty, but that sounds pretty perceptive.* And then you're more likely to hear, "Tell me more."

Using these kinds of approaches helps you initiate a conversation. It helps you build trust. And as the conversation progresses, you'll understand the appropriate time to introduce the processes and programs they can undertake to *obtain* the result. Eventually, you can teach the tools we have in the Church to help with the results they seek. But remember—that's not going to happen in the first fifteen seconds.

Words Matter—Choose Them Well

Time for a time out so I can have a word with you—literally.

Whenever you're talking to anyone about the gospel of Jesus Christ, remember that words matter. So, let's choose the right ones. Paul counseled, "Except ye utter by the tongue words easy to be understood, how shall it be known what is spoken? For ye shall speak in the air" (1 Corinthians 14:9).

Remember the principle of using language that makes sense to people (p. 82)? Thoughtful missionaries help investigators understand words that are commonly used in the Church but that don't make immediate sense to them.

Nephi might have said it best in giving us all a great example to follow: "For my soul delighteth in plainness; for after this manner doth the Lord God work among the children of men. For the Lord God giveth light onto the understanding; for he speaketh unto men according to their language, unto their understanding" (2 Nephi 31:3). You want to speak in a person's every day, common language and help them understand, just as the Lord does.

Of course, every language on earth has its peculiarities, but here I'm going to address some issues that English-speaking missionaries might encounter.

When you inform an investigator of a meeting or baptism at the stake center, he's going to hear "steak center." And he might think, *What if I'm not hungry?* or *Oh, darn, I'm a vegetarian.* Never assume that others understand the terms you use. You'd be wise to explain what a *stake center* is.

You'll also need to explain what a *ward* is because many people associate the word *ward* with a special room at a hospital. When you tell a new investigator that you want to introduce her to the ward, she's going to think, *Hold up! What kind of "church" is this, anyway?*

It's easy enough to explain. Try something like, "We have a congregational worship service each Sunday where we partake of our sacraments. The group that meets together is called a ward. The word was commonly used in Christian churches to designate a neighborhood. A group of neighbors living in a certain geographical area—a *ward*—meet together to worship." Now they get it, and it's not so strange after all.

Think of other words you might need to explain. Primary. Relief Society. Elders quorum. Testimony meeting. Fast offerings. General conference. Help investigators feel included by teaching them the vocabulary of the Church.

In addition to words peculiar to our church, you need to be aware of other commonly used words, too. Because some words you choose will inspire people to receive you better, and some words will do the opposite and are unhelpful in teaching. Representatives of Christ should never come across as overly casual, arrogant, self-centered, or interested in one-sided conversations. You want to let the investigator know by the words you use that you're focused on him and on the results *he* wants.

Let's look at the words to avoid, and the replacement words you can use instead.

Just

"Hello! We *just* wanted to present a message. . . ."

When introducing yourself or a gospel principle to someone, *just* sounds like you lack confidence: "We *just* want to tell you one thing. . . ." Sounds apologetic. Are you expecting to be rejected?

Just also sounds like what you're delivering isn't very important. It diminishes your message. "We're *just* going to share a quick scripture." Is that it? Does that make the recipient feel special? Loved? Cared for? Not really.

What's the replacement word? There isn't one. Drop *just* from your vocabulary—for the first fifteen seconds.

Tell

This one's common: "Hi, let me *tell* you about . . ." or "We're here today to *tell* you. . . ." *Tell* comes across as condescending—like the person you're talking to needs a lecture. That's even worse if you've stopped a busy person on the street. You interrupted whatever they're doing, and now you're going to give a lecture? No thanks. Teaching is not telling.

What's the replacement word? **Share. "We're here to share with you. . . ."** *Share* is warm; it suggests that you have something of meaning and value. Everybody likes someone who shares.

Inform / Explain

Two close cousins to *tell* are *inform* and *explain*. "Hi, we'd like to *inform* you about what we're doing at the local church." "Hi, let us *explain* something to you that your family really needs to know." They sound condescending. Hard to use those words, especially when you have no idea of the age, maturity, experience, or knowledge of the person to whom you're speaking. They also sound like you're winding up to deliver a lecture. And no one wants that.

Instead, use the words **involve, include,** and **invite**: **"We'd like to involve you and your family." "We'd like to include you in something that others are doing to. . . ."** People love to be involved, included, and invited. Try out some of these phrases:

"We'd like to invite you to participate in . . ."
"We invite you to enjoy with your children . . ."
"We invite you to consider . . ."

By the way, how would any of these sample sentences end? With a result! For example(s):

"We'd like to *share* with you a way to enjoy <u>quality family time</u> when it seems today that families are all going different directions."
"We'd love to *include* you and your husband in something other families are doing to maintain even greater <u>peace at home</u>."
"We want to *invite you to consider* a new family resource that's designed to <u>reduce the stresses</u> we all face when times get tough."

Continuing on: instead of tell, inform, or explain, whenever possible, use the word **conversation** to describe what you want to do. *Conversation* strongly implies participation and interaction. It lets people know that you're not at their house to dominate the evening. Instead, you want their thoughts, input, feedback, and questions. *Conversation* says we're there to interactively share.

Similarly, **discuss** or **discussion** suggests we're looking for an exchange of ideas. Yes, it's true that you are the teacher in this relationship, but it's also true that we need to listen to the viewpoint of all our investigators—because we love them. And in the end, how can we earn their trust if we don't show interest in their point of view? *Discuss* and *discussion* underscores the respect we have for all people.

Help

It's a nice thought—that you want to help people. In fact, I would hope that's a primary motivation for serving a mission. But to the person hearing it—as in, "We're here to help you"—it's a little off-putting. It implies they *need* help. Or that they're helpless. That's certainly not the impression we want to give, especially to someone we're meeting for the very first time.

The first word that gets a better reaction is **assist**, as in:

"Our hope is that as companions we can *assist* you and your girlfriend in better understanding your relationship to God and His love for each of you."

Assist doesn't suggest they're incapable of doing something or making improvements on their own. Rather, it makes them feel like they have a partner, a friend, who is going to be there with them every step of the way, arm in arm, to get the desired positive result they're seeking.

A second alternative to *help* is **support**. Try using it this way:

"Our church's purpose is to *support* those doing their best to keep a proper perspective when challenges arise." This, too, implies that we see this investigator as one trying to do what's right. They deserve our *support*.

Offer

Too often, when people are offered something, it comes with a catch. In our case, there is no catch—only promises associated with happiness.

Instead of sounding like there's something in it for us, use the word **provide**, as in, **"We would love to *provide* you and your friends a way to . . ."**; then finish the statement with a result. Now you're perceived as a provider, not a seller.

Opportunity

True enough—the gospel provides endless opportunities for all kinds of good things. So, what's wrong with the word *opportunity*? Simply put, historically speaking, it comes with too much baggage. It's too often associated with a salesperson who is self-serving—the kind people usually avoid. It's also often used in late-night infomercials to introduce a pyramid or investment scheme. When someone hears *opportunity*, he clams up right away and thinks, *Opportunity? I'd better hang on to my wallet—and run!*

What should you use instead? Well, because you're a missionary and members like to do nice things for missionaries, why don't I give you not one or two replacement words, but five! (Thank me later.) Delete *opportunity* from your vocabulary and try: **way, means, chance, resource, tool.**

So, rather than saying, "We want to offer you the opportunity," say, **"We'd like to provide you with a *way* to accomplish . . ."** and then address the desired result. Or,

"We're hoping today to provide your family a *means* by which you can achieve (result) together."

"The purpose for our being here is to provide you a *chance* to see more (result) when you're together each night."

"We've been looking forward to visiting with you this afternoon to discuss a new *resource* to help families (result)."

"To be clear, our goal is to introduce a *tool* that many young people are using now to get more (result)."

These words generate much less suspicion and more interest in your message.

We, not I

Listen to this street approach: "Hi, I want to share something with you, and I think it's going to do wonders for your family. I can't wait to tell you about it because I've been working hard on this little presentation and I'd like to give it to you right now. Can I start?"

Who's that all about?

It's all about *you*—the missionary. When you use *I*, you come across as self-centered, appearing like you want to get your numbers up or impress your companion or have something to write home about.

Instead, use **we**: **"We would like to share with you. . . ." "We're here today. . . ."**

We suggests that there are two of you representing Jesus. It also implies a larger group of believers, meaning the entire congregation. When you say, "We from The Church of Jesus Christ of Latter-day Saints," it's as though the entire community of Saints is involved in you visiting with the investigator. It means, "All of us are interested in your family. All of us are behind this." It gives you strength in numbers. People will be more confident in your message if they know others have accepted it and stand with you in delivering it.

Increase, Improve, Boost

Increase implies that there isn't enough already—that your investigator is lacking. "We want to help you increase quality time with your kids."

Improve implies that the quality is low right now—that your investigator needs fixing. "We've been sent here to help you improve your relationship with God."

Boost implies there's an insufficient quantity or quality of something your investigator needs. "We can help boost the love in your home."

None of those is going to win you any friends. You're likely to hear something like, "You know what, I don't need any of your . . . uh . . . whatever you got. Our relationships are just fine, thank you very much." Your intention was good, but your words undermined it.

Instead, try some of these to better communicate that your investigators are doing well, but you want to further the good things they're already doing:

"We're here to *strengthen* your faith even more in Jesus Christ."

"Our purpose is to further *grow* relationships within a family that are so important to every home."

"Our message is designed to *enhance* communication between friends and sustain even greater unity."

"Our hope is to further *solidify* the quality time you spend as a family."

"We're here to *expand* further on the things you're doing right now as parents to teach your kids important values."

"We want to *supplement* the great things you believe and have been taught in your own church."

Let's take a pause with that last one. The word *supplement* suggests that they're already making good choices or decisions in their life, and you just want to add to them. As President Gordon B. Hinckley once taught, "Let me say that we appreciate the truth in all churches and the good which they do. We say to the people, in effect, you bring with you all the good that you have, and then let us see if we can add to it. That is the spirit of this work. That is the essence of our missionary service" ("Excerpt from Recent Addresses of President Gordon B. Hinckley," *Ensign*, August 1998).

Your role is to supplement the good and right things investigators are already learning in their existing churches and communities because we think we can provide something to enhance or build on what they have. People are less likely to reject such a proposition.

To continue with sample benefit statements: **"We want to share how Christ's teachings will certainly *complement* the spirit we feel in your home."**

Complement means "to complete." We as missionaries are not supposed to remove the good in people; we're sent to bring them "further light and knowledge" that will complete their aim and purpose here on earth. Sadly, we as Church members too often can come across like we have it all. Like we're the only ones who have good families. Like we're the only people who teach important principles and values. Like we're the only ones who have truth. Using words, please guard against that.

In summary, let's communicate a desire to build on, add to, and support the good things someone is already doing.

And one more: **"Our goal today is to assist your family in *maintaining* the peace and harmony you've established in your home."**

As we use the word *maintain*, we are suggesting that we realize the investigator and/or their family are already doing good things. And we want to keep them on that path. *But,* you may say, *what if they're not doing good things currently in their life? Shouldn't we call them to repentance?* Well, if you want to create animosity on your first contact, go right ahead. But if your goal is to build trust, find the good in people and let them know—through the word *maintain*—that you see and recognize the positive things they *are* doing. After all, it's better to compliment people and be wrong than to criticize and be right.

Further . . . / . . . Even More

You may have also noticed that two other expressions were added to some of the sample sentences above. Those are **further** and **even more**, as in:

"We're here to *further* expand on the things you're already doing as a family to stay close." Or:

"We'd like to deliver a message that will deepen your belief in God *even more*."

Both these expressions suggest that you already know they're doing something well or admirably. These don't offend, they commend. Use them frequently—and sincerely—and conversations will flow.

Let's review the words you should be using:

- **Share**
- **Include / Involve / Invite**
- **Conversation / Discuss(ion)**
- **Assist / Support**
- **Provide**
- **Way / Means / Chance / Resource / Tool**
- **We**
- **Strengthen / Grow / Enhance / Solidify / Expand**
- **Supplement / Complement / Maintain**
- **Further . . . / . . . Even More**

All of these are much more likely to produce interest and interaction than their cousin words (tell, explain, offer, increase, improve, and so on).

Personalize Each Interaction

You have the flexibility to teach the lessons in whatever way best helps people fully prepare for their baptism and confirmation. . . .

You can teach the lessons in many ways. Which lesson you teach, when you teach it, and how much time you give to it are best determined by the needs of the person you are teaching and the direction of the Spirit. Do not memorize the entire lesson. (*Preach My Gospel*, vii)

As we've already discussed, the Lord has provided further direction in recent years and instructed preachers of His gospel to avoid rote presentations that can come across with the stale sound of someone else's script. To assist you in achieving a sense of newness with everyone with whom you speak, we will work to personalize every contact.

Here are some suggestions on how to make every approach (benefit statement) sound unique to each person:

Focus on Results—A Disservice If You Don't

When you knock on doors or approach someone on the street corner, you're not fulfilling an obligation to yourself or trying to please your mission leaders. Instead, when done in the spirit of true missionary work, you're focusing on a way to serve by helping someone achieve results that are not only important to them but necessary for their salvation. As you try to communicate that, using the word **disservice** can help:

"We chose to come here today because we felt it would be a *disservice* if we didn't invite you to participate in something we believe could bless your life."

"We believe it would be a *disservice* if we didn't include you in something we believe will really enhance your relationships with friends."

The word *disservice* reflects two mentalities all missionaries should possess. First, *dis-* suggests that we don't want to leave anyone out; and second, *-service* says exactly what we're here to do: serve our fellowmen. When someone is approached using that word, they are less likely to be perturbed or afraid, and more likely to see you as someone who is there to benefit them. *Disservice* sounds friendly, thoughtful, and based on good intentions.

Communicate Eagerness, Not Anxiousness

Unlike a salesperson that may be required to hit quotas, righteous missionaries have an urgency because it benefits the investigator, not the missionaries. As such, we should use words and expressions that let people know we are—and have been—waiting to serve and teach them. Here are some examples:

"We've been *looking forward* to meeting you."
"We've been *eager* to speak with you."
"We've been *excited* to come to your home."
"We *couldn't wait* to see your office."
"We've been *hoping* for the chance to have a brief conversation with you."

These types of phrases say, "You're not just Contact #63 today. No, we've been led to you. We believe we're here for a purpose." You want to let them know that you couldn't wait to get here—that knocking on this door was the result of divine inspiration, not the result of trying to fill numbers or wrap up an assignment.

Whenever Possible, Thank or Compliment

As ambassadors of Christ, missionaries should be the politest people in town. And since everyone appreciates a sincere thank you or compliment, when appropriate, think of a way you can demonstrate Christlike regard for those you meet by either starting your benefit statement with a thank you (**"We appreciate the things we've heard about your family"**), or a compliment (**"We understand you're one of the best volunteers at the school"**).

It's difficult for people to feel negatively toward someone who is genuinely cordial and considerate. Yes, there will always be ornery people in this world, but your example of Christlike kindness helps to immediately invite the Spirit and set the tone for what should be a warm conversation.

Give a Time Frame

You'll recall that in Chapter Three we pointed out that results begin for an investigator *as soon as he decides* to make a commitment—even a small one. Therefore, when you deliver a benefit statement, don't hesitate to let him know that the result you're introducing can be achieved or obtained sooner rather than later.

For instance, you might say, **"Tyler, we're excited to share with you a message tonight that could change your outlook on that difficult work situation as quickly as *tomorrow morning* when you get back to the office."**

Or, **"Susan, if you'll allow us to stop by this afternoon, we have something we'd like to share that we're certain will give you a new perspective as *the holidays approach*."**

In both these examples—and the ones you should develop yourself—you'll notice that they provide immediate, or at least quick, hope. Those you teach need to know that blessings await anyone who will change (repent) and turn to Christ and His gospel. Why should they delay obtaining blessings (results) when they're right there for the receiving?

Make sure the time frame is realistic and within reach. If it's too far out, they can more easily resist your invitation and tell you to check back with them at some future date. If that happens, they're delaying or deferring results for another day! That's unfortunate.

God wants to bless His children if they will just turn to Him:

> And, behold, there was a woman which had a spirit of infirmity eighteen years, and was bowed together, and could in no wise lift up herself.
>
> And when Jesus saw her, he called her to him, and said unto her, Woman, thou art loosed from thine infirmity.
>
> And he laid his hands on her; and *immediately* she was made straight, and glorified God. (Luke 13:11–13; emphasis added)

A time frame could be this hour, this day, this week, or this month. But to suggest blessings won't come until later down the road—such as, at baptism—is to question God's abilities and deny investigators the results the gospel can bring them instantly. So, whatever the time period, don't make them think they have to wait until summer. Or until next month. Or even next week. Lots of results can be achieved this week, today, this afternoon *when your kids get home from school,* or *this evening at dinner with your family.*

Allude to a Success Story

Before you go see a movie or try out a new restaurant, what are we all likely to do? Check out the reviews, of course! Few of us venture into unchartered territory. We're usually disinclined to take chances or suffer the consequences of risk.

Well, investigators are no different—especially when it comes to exploring a new religion, a new lifestyle, a different circle of friends. To help ease the uncertainty, missionaries will relate success stories whenever meeting or teaching a new investigator.

You see, people love success stories. They're like reviews on Yelp or third-party testimonials. If we can report situations where others are giving our Church and the benefit of its teachings four or five stars, so to speak, new investigators are more likely to cut you some slack and give you a shot.

Keep in mind, though, that in this case we're talking about using a success story within the benefit statement. Which means it needs to be brief. Very brief. Save the details for later. All we're attempting to convey at this point is that we have something relevant to the investigator based on the fact that others in similar situations are benefiting, too. Success stories let people know you're there because of success others are seeing and experiencing, not because we desire to find our first successful example.

Here are some samples of success stories used in a benefit statement:

"We came to your home today because we just had another wonderful conversation with your neighbor, Lloyd . . ."

"As we were passing and saw you and your kids playing, we felt we should stop and share with you a brief message that several

families in the community are telling us has been helpful as they're raising children."

"We wanted to phone you first thing this morning because other students we're meeting with on campus are reporting great results from our message, and we didn't want another day to pass before getting a chance to share it with you, as well."

If success stories inspire people in their everyday lives to try something they might not otherwise try (such as a product or a movie or a restaurant), with your efforts it can also work to encourage people to meet with the Lord's missionaries.

Highlight Their Location

Consider singling out or making your investigator feel special by referencing their location. Here's an example:

"The reason we're specifically here in this neighborhood today is. . . ." Then continue with a success story from that neighborhood.

"We've been getting a lot of positive feedback from families in this particular part of the community–and because of that interest, we didn't want to return home tonight until we knocked on your door and shared with you the same message others are receiving so well."

Help people feel special because of where they live, work, or gather. Help them feel part of an exclusive group. Sure, you could be on any street in this huge metropolitan area. But tonight, prayerfully, you're standing on *this* corner in their particular part of the community.

Indicate Inspiration

When appropriate, don't hide the fact that you were led to their location by inspiration: **"We're not sure why, but we felt impressed to come and knock on your door tonight and share a message with you about. . . ."**

Don't say it just to say it. But when you *do* feel inspired, share it! Don't you agree it will get someone's attention when they know the Holy Ghost has led you to them? It's not unreasonable to think that your inspiration was the result of *their* prayers—silent or vocal. And if nothing else, it will certainly help one of Heavenly Father's children know that they are loved.

Be sincere and authentic in telling them that you let the Spirit guide you—that the Spirit can inspire you where to go and who to approach. Don't hide that; it should never be a secret that your actions are guided by the Spirit.

Of course, always be honest. Whatever happens, never fool people by saying you were led by inspiration if you weren't.

Mention You're a Minister

As appropriate, gently share with people that you're acting as an ordained minister of Jesus Christ. You're not simply a volunteer. To the secular world, a volunteer is someone who gives up some time. It's true that you're giving up time, but that's not all. As an ordained minister, you've been set apart from the world to proclaim His message. When people know you're an ordained messenger of God, they're likely to treat you and your message more seriously.

So, Then What?

Let's say that you've gone through your introduction—or benefit statement—properly. That is, you've:

1. **Introduced yourself and your companion;**
2. **Said who or what you represent; and**
3. **Briefly explained the benefit (or result) they will receive by talking with you.**

Now, how might that person respond? That's hard to predict because it depends on so many factors—many of them outside of your control. For instance, if they're putting the kids to bed, or finishing up a phone call to their parents across the country, or walking out of their apartment on the way to the store, their reply could be something as simple as, "I wish I could talk, but now's not a good time."

Did you hear that? They "wish they could talk"! *That's* a good sign. Responsible missionaries will make a note of it and plan to come back.

Face it, you're never going to hear someone say, "Where have you been? I've been waiting for you to come! I've got an oversized bathtub in the backyard. Baptize me now!" (Some people might very well say they've been anticipating your arrival, but honestly—an oversized tub?)

In most cases, if your introduction has been done well and with sincerity, you will hear a response like "What do you mean, exactly?" or "That's interesting," or "Oh, yeah?" or even, "Hmm." In other words, though their response may seem unenthusiastic on the outside, on the inside something is prompting them to hear more. Rather than admit instant interest, though, typically investigators will act like, well, investigators: interested, but cynical. Curious for truth, but suspicious of those who claim it. So, be glad their reply wasn't "Get lost!" and assume their awkward reaction reflects a degree of interest.

What do you do next? Do you launch into your message? Do you roll up your sleeves, grab a chair, and dive into a lesson? Sure, if the Spirit directs you to. He is, after all, your best trainer.

More likely, though, you should resist the temptation to instantly start teaching a person whose needs are still unclear, and say something like:

"Before we share our thoughts, we'd love to better understand your [fill in the blank]."

What *would* you like to better understand? If you used a benefit statement, continue down that path and name a topic that relates to the result you just introduced. For example, if your benefit statement addressed "harmony in the home," you might say, **"Before we share our thoughts, we'd love to better understand your [family]."** Since "family" and "harmony in the home" are related, their family is an obvious topic you want to "better understand."

Or, if your benefit statement addressed "better appreciating our relationship to God as His children," you then might say, **"Before we share our thoughts, we'd appreciate understanding better your [general views about God]."** See how they relate?

When explaining that your interest isn't just in talking, but in listening to the investigator, you're establishing a relationship based on mutual respect. "Each person or family you teach is unique. Even though you will not understand all of their interests, achievements, needs, and concerns, you should seek to be sensitive to their circumstances" (*Preach My Gospel*, 179).

As you express a desire to know them as much as to teach them, you will then be in a better place to follow your last statement (". . . we'd appreciate better understanding your [blank]"), with:

"Would that be all right?"

In other words, you're seeking permission to continue—not so much to continue a sermon, but to continue by learning about them. Yep, you're about to ask some questions. You're not there to give a scripted presentation; you're there to tailor your message for them. And to do that, you need to gather some information about them.

You see, your presentation is not memorized. You're not delivering it repetitiously. You're saying that you care about them and that you want to help first by listening to them. And you're indicating *We're not here just to do all the talking. We're here to interact. We're here to have a dialogue with you, not to monologue on your doorstep.*

But let's go back to that last question, "Would that be all right?" In most cases, their response will be "Yeah," "Sure," or "Okay."

There are several reasons they're agreeable at this point. First, your introduction was simple, clear, and respectful. Next, you offered up a desirable result that could be theirs if they would commit a few moments of their time to you. And third, you told them you want to "better understand" them. As we'll discuss in a later chapter, everyone wants to be understood. The opposite is to be misunderstood, and few things can be more frustrating, aggravating, and troubling to people.

By telling them that your first priority is to understand them, they immediately see you as someone different. You're not like the last stranger who appeared at their door, trying to sell them something they didn't want or need. You bring a special feeling because you are representing the Savior, Jesus Christ. And is there anyone in the history of the world who has shown more interest in others than Him?

Of course, not all will allow you to continue. They can exercise their agency and refuse. But if they do agree ("Yeah," "Sure," "Okay"), they're giving you permission to continue, to ask them questions. A dialogue has begun. And teaching can now take place.

Benefit Statements for the Ward Council and Missionary Coordination

Believe it or not, you should be just as careful about using a benefit statement when introducing yourself at a ward council (or any other committee in the ward or branch where you serve). The way you introduce yourself on that first Sunday is a key moment because members, as much as they're taught not to judge others, will instantly do just that—and right then you will begin to build either trust or mistrust.

Based on the first words out of your mouth, members of the ward council will decide whether you're the right missionary for the ward. Whether you're serious about teaching the gospel. Whether you even know that much about the gospel. Whether you're truly committed. Whether you're friendly enough to do the job.

No pressure.

What on earth should you say? How about something like:

"Hello, my name is Elder Dickson. I'm from Colorado. I'm very grateful to be a part of this ward and to serve side by side with each of you in sharing the gospel message with our friends and neighbors in the community."

That shows you're excited to be there.

You might even say (if you can do so honestly), **"I've heard a lot of great things about this ward."** Or, **"I've been hoping to be called to this particular part of the mission. My wish has come true!"** These introductions help build rapport. They help establish trust. Because these people, who care deeply about their ward, neighborhoods, and community, will feel they have a new ally in the gathering of Israel, someone who is as deeply committed to the success of the ward—not to mention their friends' and families' happiness—as they are.

Help them remember you long after the meeting. "Boy, did you see the way that elder introduced himself? We have a dedicated missionary on our hands. I can't wait to work with him." And in the back of his mind he's thinking, *I can just imagine this missionary working with the Goodall family next door. I have total confidence he can handle himself and he's not going to embarrass me.*

With that, you're on your way to a very productive transfer.

Let's look at the opposite: when the bishop invites you to introduce yourself, you say, "Hi. Yeah, I'm the new missionary in the ward. I've got about three months left. Let me know if you need my help. So . . . yeah. Oh, and while I'm thinking about it, who's got the dinner calendar?" That's a fifteen-second benefit statement, all right—but it's only to benefit you. Sounds like a missionary who's going to go very hungry each night around dinnertime.

Benefit Statements for Ward and Stake Members

Members of wards, branches, and stakes where you'll be serving want to trust you. They want to believe that you are going to take good care of the people they introduce to you—their friends and family. They want to know you're not going to misrepresent the things they've already shared with the special people in their lives. They want to know you're not going to mess up what they've told people missionaries are all about. Simply put, they don't want to be embarrassed.

When you introduce yourself for the first time in a ward or branch, an audience of anywhere between a dozen and hundreds of people will immediately decide if you're someone they can trust.

To be effective as a missionary with ward members, you must let them know you're excited to teach the gospel to their neighbors and friends in the community—because your role is to teach. You don't want them thinking you transferred here grudgingly and you're just biding time until the next transfer. Communicate with words and actions that show you see yourself as a member of their community. This is *your* home, too.

And unlike the nonmember on the street, ward members want to know where you're from. Tell them. And they're curious about your family. Share with them.

When you're invited to introduce yourself in sacrament meeting or Sunday School or priesthood meeting or Relief Society, say something like:

"Hello, my name is Sister Craig. I'm from Dayton, Ohio, and I have three brothers and sisters. I've been on my mission for about a year, and I'm excited to meet all of you and do whatever I can to earn your trust, so together my companion and I can teach your friends in your home."

Set expectations. Establish your role in the ward—to teach the gospel. You're also establishing their role as ward members—to introduce investigators to you. And you're doing it all in a friendly, non-pushy way, letting them know you can't wait to get started sharing the gospel in this area.

You can mix this up any way that suits your personality; it's the principle of what you're saying that matters most. You want to let them know that they can achieve greater unity in their community because friends and family are listening to the gospel. You *don't* want them to think that you merely followed the instructions of the transfer, will be here for a few months, and then ship out.

No, you want to impress upon them that right now, they're your top priority. And you'll do everything in your power to help them succeed in spreading the gospel while participating in the gathering here in their part of the vineyard.

Wouldn't it be helpful to the work if members actually viewed you as their "hope of Israel"?

Chapter Six

Skill 2: Assessing for Understanding

**"Wherefore, my beloved brethren, let every
man be swift to hear, slow to speak."**

James, brother of Jesus, James 1:19

As a missionary, you will adjust your teaching to meet the singular situation of your investigator. "Each person or family you teach is unique. Even though you will not understand all of their interests, achievements, needs, and concerns, you should seek to be sensitive to their circumstances" (*Preach My Gospel*, 179).

In order to do that, you need to do your best to skillfully assess—and listen to—the **interests**, **achievements**, **needs**, and **concerns** related to their circumstances.

As in all other things, Jesus "often asked questions to help people ponder and apply principles" (*Preach My Gospel*, 183). Jesus, of course, was the Master Teacher. He knew when it was time to teach, but He also knew when it was time to assess and listen. One of the ways He assessed was through thoughtful questioning—and you can do the same.

If you want to be able to assess, you need to ask the right kinds—and amount—of questions. "Asking too many questions, especially in your first visit, gives the impression that you are conducting an 'interrogation.' Do not ask people to give specific answers about unimportant or obvious details. This will turn a good teaching environment into a game of guessing" (*Preach My Gospel*, 186).

To see what that means, and to get an idea of the wrong kinds of questions, imagine a conversation between a missionary and a woman he and his companion just met knocking on doors.

Missionary: Hi, how's it going today?

Woman: Pretty good.

Missionary: Good, good. So, you lived here long?

Woman: Yeah. My whole life.

Missionary: Okay, terrific. Um . . . so, are these your kids? (She's holding one with two others wrapped around her legs.)

Woman: Yes, they're . . . all of them, all five.

Missionary: Wow! Huh. Okay. Five! So, you like children?

Woman: (She just looks at him.)

Missionary: Hmm, okay. Uh, so, uh, so what does your husband do?

Woman: He's a long-haul carrier. He drives a truck.

Missionary: Truck driver. Excellent. Okay. Uh, I bet he's gone a lot.

Woman: Uh-huh, all the time.

Missionary: Sure. Um. So, you have any hobbies?

Woman: If you call taking care of kids a hobby. I don't have a lot of time to do much else.

Missionary: Ooh. Okay, that's too bad. So, hey, you ever . . . , you ever go to church?

Woman: Church? No, not with five kids—all twelve and under.

Missionary: Oh, yeah. Okay. Well. Joseph Smith. That name ring a bell for you?

Woman: Um, yeah. Knew a guy named Joe Smith. Used to work at the power company.

Missionary: No, well. . . . Right. Probably a different Joseph Smith. I'm talking about the prophet. We can talk about him maybe some other time. But, um, so, uh, let's see. Uh, listen, if I could share with you how modern-day prophets have actually opened up the world to eternal families, if you could have all of these kids with you forever and live in this type of happy family state eternally, do think that'd be of interest to you?

Woman: I wouldn't want to live like this for eternity; eternity's a really long time.

Missionary [sighs and turns to his companion]: Okay, uh, Elder, you wanna take it from here?

***

Good times.

Let's review that painful dialogue. How many questions did the missionary ask? You don't need to count—just know that he asked a *lot* of questions. Were they productive and helpful? Not really. Maybe the opposite.

What else was wrong with his questions? First, there wasn't much sincerity or care behind them. He showed little empathy. Here's a woman who is at home almost all the time with five kids twelve and under and without her husband's help. The missionary didn't even *react* to that.

That's not all. He wasn't really listening to her answers. It was like he had a memorized list of questions to plow through so that he could launch into his memorized presentation.

This is a bit of an exaggerated example, but do you ever wonder why investigators don't give missionaries their full attention when they're being asked questions? Usually it's because the questions don't relate to them. Or, they know the missionaries aren't really listening to their answers, so there's no point in responding with any kind of substance.

Assessing is *not* asking twenty questions. It's *not* interrogating someone. Instead, it's a tool that builds trust through thoughtful empathy and connection. Assessing establishes the groundwork for you to share a tailored message designed specifically for that person's or family's circumstances.

Once again, to really assess, do all you can to determine a person's **interests**, **achievements**, **needs**, and **concerns** (not necessarily in that order). As stated earlier in *Preach My Gospel*, you probably won't have the opportunity to understand all these things, but a humble and honest attempt to do so will further strengthen the investigator's trust in you.

Let's take a look at **needs** first, and how those might be assessed.

Did the woman in the above example express any needs? She sure did—maybe not in exact words, but she told the missionary that her husband's not there a lot, she has a gaggle of kids, she clearly doesn't have time for herself, she doesn't seem interested in eternity with her family (at least not like *this*), and she doesn't seem to have another adult she can to talk to or confide in. Having heard all those things, you could accurately guess that she needs family unity, purpose and meaning in her life, and empathetic adult interaction on non-trivial topics. Notice that all those things are available through the Church of Jesus Christ of Latter-day Saints and the gospel we preach.

So, you've probably identified her likely needs. What, then, are her **interests**? What does she wish for, hope for? Interests are likes and wants. They're different from needs. Again, once understood, they help you better tailor a message for her.

Based on the conversation you read, can you figure out what potential interests she might have? Maybe she'd like to join a play group with other mothers. Maybe she would want some babysitters. Maybe she'd enjoy some women friends she could talk to and spend time with.

Aha. Would the Church have any ways to address those interests? Some of the Young Women might be able to help with babysitting. Primary could provide her a nice break from her children—while giving them some fun activities and music time to reinforce values she hopes they acquire. And she could find great benefit in attending Relief Society, where she could spend time with other women in similar circumstances. Suddenly she could have a support network of women friends who empathize with and understand her.

Let's not stop there. We've only touched on two of the four things we should assess. Are there other **concerns** this woman might have, based on what she said? It seems the family doesn't have much time together; the father is always gone, on the road as a truck driver. Might she be concerned for his safety and welfare? Could she be concerned that her kids are missing their dad? Or that they aren't getting enough time with him to establish healthy relationships? Could there be a financial concern, causing her husband to work nonstop? Is she concerned for her kids' physical or mental health—or even her own?

And though the husband wasn't part of the conversation, are there things you can assess about *him*? (Assessing is not judging; it's just assessing.) He might feel unhappy that he is away from his family so much and so often. He may feel that he has far less time with his wife than he wants. While he is out on the road, he may be feeling guilty that his wife is back home being lonely, burdened, and overwhelmed. And he could be feeling the same.

This isn't to suggest that all is doom and gloom with this family— after all, we're only seeing a snapshot of her life in a singular moment in time. Let's not forget that there are signs of **achievements**, as well.

She is, very importantly, a mother. She's caring for her kids and presumably doing all she can in these circumstances to nourish and foster their growth and protection. And, as we observed, the kids are clinging to her, so that suggests a closeness they feel to their mom. We can also assume this woman is friendly, since she did answer the door and carried on a conversation with two young men while tending to her children. Of course, we shouldn't ignore the fact that despite what sounds like a challenging employment situation, this husband and wife are married and loyal to one another. These are all noteworthy accomplishments, for sure!

If you were the missionary in this situation, what else would you want to learn about this woman and her circumstances that could help you prepare a message that would speak directly to the results she needs in her life?

You might ask about her upbringing. Does she have family in the area? What about extended family? How is her relationship with them? Do they provide any support? What activities do they do together? Are they religious people? Do they believe in Christ? Do they claim a church? Does this woman pray? Does she teach her children about Jesus?

The answers to these and many other questions can give you a fuller picture of the interests, achievements, needs, and concerns of the person with whom you are interacting. By no means should you ask all such questions at once. While we will cover shortly *how* you can skillfully ask these types of questions, be judicious and thoughtful in *when* you ask questions, too. Some are more personal than others— and if you haven't established trust, you're more likely to push the person away because you'll come across as inappropriately probing and prying.

There are some things you can infer just from the place you're serving. For example, I was a missionary in Japan, where many people had no concept of a Savior. They'd hardly heard of Jesus Christ. They barely even understood what a god was. Joseph Smith and the Restoration? Not even. In trying to tailor our message to these people, therefore, we usually started with the concept of a loving Heavenly Father, what that means, and why it's the basis of everything else that's important in life. What are some fair assumptions you can gain from the area where you're serving?

Four Assessing Techniques

To assist you in becoming a more skilled assessor, let's look at four techniques that, when used together, will aid your ability to learn what's most important and helpful (to you) about every investigator. These four techniques are:

1. **Relevant Topics**
2. **Ten Serving Words**
3. **Five Magical Phrases**
4. **Conversation Starters**

Again, these are not intended to be stand-alone techniques. They are most effective if used collectively when assessing an individual or a family. Don't judge each on its own; rather, you'll soon see how, when properly combined, they become super helpful in carrying on natural conversations of assessing.

1. Relevant Topics

It's important to get relevant information from investigators, but how can you do that without asking a bunch of questions that simply make them feel like they're sitting in a dark room with a light bulb swaying over their head? Start with relevant topics, because that will help you better know the investigator's interests, achievements, needs, and concerns.

What are some relevant topics you should explore and uncover about investigators? Here are some examples (in no specific order):

Living Conditions

It would be helpful to learn a little bit about an investigator's home life. Who resides in the home? Do they live with relatives? Knowing whether they rent or own would give you some insights into their situation. It might indicate the length of time they have lived in the area and the potential stability of their living situation for the future. Are they expecting a transfer that will necessitate a move? You wouldn't necessarily ask detailed questions, but if you know—even by observation or listening to off-handed comments—a little about their living conditions, it can help you better understand the person or family.

Career

An occupation can tell you a lot about people. Do they work with family—and how does that affect family relationships? Do they travel much, and if so, what impact does that have on their family life? Do they work nine to five, with little or a lot of overtime? Do they work on Sundays? If so, how does that affect family time? Is one spouse coming home from work when the other is leaving? These are factors and challenges you should be sensitive to.

A career can also tell you a lot about how to teach someone. Can you use examples or metaphors from their professional field to explain things more effectively? Absolutely.

Lifestyle and Personality

Hints about these two relevant topics may come from careful observation instead of questions. You may observe (without snooping!) the books on the bookshelf in the family room and understand that this person loves history. Is that helpful for you to know? Of course—it may be of interest that the Book of Mormon is an historical religious record or that the Church has been celebrating the 200th anniversary of a significant event. Or you might learn from trophies or other memorabilia that this guy is really into youth sports. He coaches his kids' teams and is constantly involved in that. What does that tell you about the importance of family?

Future Plans

You might ask, "Where do you see your family in the next year? In the next five years?" Or you might ask, "Are you putting down roots here?" They might respond, "Oh, no, we intend to move back to South Carolina as soon as we get a chance because our family's there. We really want to be close to relatives." That's a great insight that tells you a lot about what's important to these people.

Or a husband might reply, "We've lived in seven states in six years because of the nature of my work. I'm not sure where we're going to be a year from now." This can give you a glimpse into their needs and/or concerns as a family.

Education

Someone might say, "We feel education is so important that we're already establishing college funds for our toddlers. We want them all to get their master's degree by the time they're twenty-four. In fact, we expect most of them to get doctorates, just like their aunts and uncles."

Does that give you some good insights into how you might tailor your teaching? Definitely. Think of all the times prophets have emphasized education, encouraged young people to gain advanced education, and inspired older people to continue their learning. The Church's emphasis on education is also evidenced by its universities and BYU-Pathway Worldwide. All that would be relevant to this family, as would the many scriptures on learning in the Doctrine and Covenants (see as examples D&C 90:15; 88:118; 109:7; 130:19). Of course, the importance of serving missions might be considered a plus or minus to this investigator family, so at least now you can be sensitive to it when sharing thoughts about your own mission experience and your time away from a formal education.

Upbringing

What was important to them in their home when they were being raised? What kind of family situation did they come from? What kind of parents do they have? Was it a single-parent situation, or did they have a strong mother/father presence in their home? All these are relevant to the way they might view the world and the family unit and will determine whether certain elements of your message will resonate with them.

Personal Value System

Learning the personal value system (the way they look at the world and the people in it) of those you teach can give you great insights into them as people and which values taught by the Church you might want to emphasize—and which might be more difficult to accept. A personal value system can also indicate their spirituality and how it has shaped their thinking.

Health

When an investigator says, "Our daughter just got out of the hospital where she was being treated for a congenital heart defect," you have a basis for teaching, at some point, the power of faith and the power of the priesthood. Depending on what health concerns a family has, you might want to teach the principles behind the commandments, including the Word of Wisdom.

Mortality

How do they view life? Have they ever given any thought to their purpose on earth and what it all means? Perhaps you learn that they've recently had a death in the family. Or there has been a marriage. Maybe someone's expecting a baby. All of this gives you information that can better prepare you for teaching opportunities.

Hobbies

What do they do for entertainment? A father might say, "You know, there's this new suspense thriller out, and we can't wait to go see it. My twelve-year-old, he's a big fan of scary movies." This kind of information can offer helpful hints about who you're teaching and what you might teach them.

Religious Background and Church Experience

What do they know about Jesus Christ? Do they have a Bible in their home, and do they read it? How often? Do they refer to it? If so, perhaps you could use it when you share key scriptures with them. Learning about their church experience—including their reception to pastoral or ministerial authority—will broaden your understanding of your investigators and how to best teach them.

Traditions

Do they do a lot at the holidays, or are holidays downplayed—or even disfavored? A retiree might say, "We're certainly not looking forward to having the disruption of our kids and grandchildren being here." That will tell you a lot about how they view their family relationships. So will other questions about holiday traditions: "What does your family typically do for Christmas or Easter or Thanksgiving?" You might ask a single person, "What are your plans for the holidays?" If she replies, "Nothin' much," and says she doesn't visit family or friends, you can get some great information on what she's thinking and what she might need.

***

These few topics only scratch the surface of what might be relevant in better understanding the people you teach. And it all hinges on listening, perceiving, and being in tune with the Spirit. Your purpose in exploring topics is to gather as much information as possible on the people you teach. Total assessment rarely happens in one meeting or one discussion, especially since you don't want to exhaust anyone with your questions. It often takes place over the course of several meetings with the same investigator as the relationship grows.

Of course, member missionaries can be extremely valuable in providing some of these insights for you, and you should not hesitate to ask the member about their neighbor or relative before the first meeting. In fact, you *should* do it! This demonstrates thoughtful preparation that will only increase the members' trust in you, the set-apart teacher of their valued relative or friend.

The main thing that will jeopardize your ability to assess effectively is your lack of interest in others. If you really don't want to hear about them and you just want to talk, here's what you're saying, in effect: "Shh—be quiet, I practiced all morning for this lesson, and I want to teach it before I forget it. Everybody ready?"

That kind of rushed insensitivity will prevent you from becoming a good assessor. It will also most assuredly cause investigators to lose trust in you, meaning your message will fall on deaf ears. You've probably heard the popular saying, "People don't care how much you know, until they know how much you care." That couldn't be truer when it comes to teaching the gospel of Jesus Christ.

2. Ten Serving Words

Let me introduce you to ten words you use every day, probably without much thought. They are simple words—questions, really—that will serve you and your investigator well. Here they are:

1. **Who**
2. **What**
3. **Where**
4. **When**

5. **Which**
6. **Why**
7. **How**

"Wait," you say. "That's only seven."

The others are combinations:

8. **How much**
9. **How many**
10. **How often**

By utilizing these words to ask questions, you'll discover a wealth of information.

A few cautions: *where* doesn't always mean a geographic location, like "Where are you from originally?" While that's helpful, *where* could also be used this way: "Where are you seeing the biggest change in your son since he started hanging out with that group of boys?"

Why, I think you'll find, is usually the hardest of the ten. That doesn't mean you shouldn't use it; it just should never sound like you're looking down your nose at an answer. It's simply a follow-up question after they've shared something with you ("Why do you think your kids like going to church when they visit their grandparents?").

How is usually exploring a process ("How do you decide as a family . . . ?"), except in the "combination" words—then you're looking for a quantity ("How much? - Twelve pounds"; "How many - Three kids"; "How often - Every other week").

The Ten Serving Words are used with a relevant topic. To see how it's done, let's practice with one of the relevant topics we discussed earlier: **Mortality**, or **the purpose of life**. Here are some questions you could ask. (Keep in mind, none of these are absolutely-you-gotta-use-these-or-you'll-never-be-an-effective-missionary questions. They're simply examples that could be used in different situations and in any order.)

- *Who* **in the past has taught you about your relationship with God?**
- *What* **is your view of our purpose on earth?**

- *Where* do you think we go when this life experience is over?
- *When* did you come to that realization?
- *Which* of your parents had the most influence on your beliefs?
- *Why* do you think it's so important to ask ourselves where we came from and where we're going when life is over?
- *How* are you attempting to teach this to your children?
- *How much* does your view of life's purpose guide your daily choices?
- *How many* times have you thought to ask God for answers to these questions?
- *How often* is this topic discussed here in your home?

Certainly, not all these questions are necessary, but by using as many of the Ten Serving Words as is appropriate, you will obtain valuable information to guide your teaching.

Next, let's practice with the relevant topic of **hobbies**. You might ask:

- *Who* in your family plays the piano?
- *What* hobbies do you or your spouse enjoy together?
- *Where* did you get to be so good at (hobby)?
- *When* do you find the time to engage in (hobby) with your busy schedule?
- *Which* one of you is the most talented at (hobby)?
- *Why* do you enjoy (hobby) so much?
- *How* do you involve your family in your hobby, or is it something you prefer to do on your own?
- *How much* time did it take to reach this skill level?
- *How many* of your friends enjoy (hobby) with you?
- *How often* do you engage in this hobby–every week or monthly?

How about the relevant topic of **values**?

- *Who* usually takes the lead in teaching these values to your kids–you or your wife?
- *What* do you think are the most important values we need to teach kids today?
- *Where* do you think values have declined the most in society–schools? The community? Entertainment?
- *When* was a recent time you were able to sit down with your kids and share your thoughts on this topic in a way they really understood?
- *Which* issue facing society today do you think is the biggest threat to families?
- *Why* do you think it's important to spend time teaching children proper values, especially at home?
- *How* do you think religion or the right church might help you teach good values to your kids?
- *How much* do you find your values are in synch with your friends' or neighbors' values?
- *How many* times since school started have your values conflicted with those of your classmates?
- *How often* have you had to defend your values at school?

Again, are all those questions necessary? No. Nor are they intended to be in any specific or correct order. You'll use some like these in one situation, others in another. But you get the idea of how these ten words can help you ask questions that are relevant to the interests, achievements, needs, and concerns of your investigators.

Take some time to practice the Ten Serving Words. Have a family member, friend, or even your companion give you a relevant topic, then ask the ten appropriate questions. For the sake of the exercise, your partner doesn't need to role-play answering your questions; it's more important that you gain a comfort level and proficiency in asking relevant questions on just about any topic.

3. Five Magical Phrases

The next step in becoming more skilled at assessing people is to use five exceptional phrases on top of the relevant topics and Ten Serving Words. These "Magical" (because they're so simple yet effective) Phrases are:

1. **Tell me . . .**
2. **Describe for me . . .**
3. **Share with me . . .**
4. **What do you think . . .**
5. **What has been your experience . . .**

Let's take a look at how they work.

You begin by using one of the Magical Phrases to introduce a relevant topic. But you don't stop there. Immediately after you bring up the relevant topic, you ask any *two* of the Ten Serving Words. A more complete and helpful answer will then follow from your investigator.

Let's try some.

Tell Me (Us) About . . .

Start this phrase with any relevant topic.

Here's an example: "Tell me about your job." But remember, don't stop there. Here's what will happen if you do:

> Missionary: "So, tell me about your job."
> Investigator: "I'm a farmer."
> Missionary: "Oh, you're a farmer. Okay. Have you been doing that long?"
> Investigator: "About twenty-five years."
> Missionary: "Do you enjoy it?"
> Investigator: "Sure."
> Missionary: "Yeah. Does your family farm with you?"
> Investigator: "Nope. They all moved away."
> Missionary: "Oh, great. Um, did they farm with you before they left?"
> Investigator: "That's probably why they left."
> Missionary: "Ssssuper. So, not to change subjects, but have you ever seen one of our temples?"

***

What just happened? An awkward back and forth, that's what happened. The investigator only gave short—though important—answers. Why? Because the missionary wasn't asking effectively.

To his credit, the missionary *did* begin with a Magical Phrase and a good, relevant topic ("Tell me about your job.") But after that, because he didn't follow up with two of the Ten Serving Words, the conversation fell flat. (There's another reason, too, but we'll cover that a little later.)

To repeat, what can we do to improve our questioning? Put a mental semicolon after "Tell me about your job" and add a couple of the Ten Serving Words. Here's how that would work: **"Tell me about your job; *what* got you interested in that line of work, and *when* did you first start?"**

More examples:

"Tell me about your studies; *which* school you attend, and *how* you selected your major."

"Tell us about religion in your life; *how* has it impacted your family, and *why* do you think it's so important to raise kids with Christian beliefs?"

Will you get one-word answers with this kind of questioning? No. It's impossible. It invites the person to openly describe more of herself and her thinking. You create a situation in which the person wants to expound. One-word answers may give you data, but they don't provide much insight. By getting people to elaborate, you'll get information that will help you better understand their interests, their achievements, their needs, and their concerns.

Describe for Me (Us) . . .

You're going to use this phrase the same way—with a relevant topic, followed by a couple of the Ten Serving Words. Again, stick to one topic within each phrase. Check out some examples:

"Describe for us the relationships you have with your neighbors; *how many* do you normally socialize with, and *what* kind of activities do you like to do when you get together?"

"Describe for me your background; *where* you were raised, and *when* you moved to this area."

"Describe for us your interactions with members of the Latter-day Saint community; *who* do you know that goes to our church, and *what* have they shared with you about our beliefs?"

Share with Me (Us) . . .

This one works the same way as the first two. Follow this phrase with a relevant topic and a couple of the Ten Serving Words:

"Share with us how you two met; *how many* years you've been together, and *how* religion has played a role in your relationship."

"Share with me a little about your church attendance; *when* did you first start going to that church, and *what* does it provide that you particularly like?"

"Share with us what you know about the Prophet Joseph Smith; *where* did you first hear about him, and *what* are your impressions?"

What Do You Think . . .

This is an especially effective phrase because people *love* to tell you their opinion or what they think—when asked sincerely. You get how it works—Phrase, topic, Serving words—so consider these examples:

"What do you think about the youth group your kids attend? *Which* church sponsors it, and *what* are some of the activities they provide?"

"What do you think about organized religion as a way to reinforce the values you're teaching your kids? *How many* times do you think you've attended this year, and *what* kind of experiences do you have when you go?"

"What do you think about the Latter-day Saints at your work or school? *How* would you characterize them and their lifestyle, and *when's* the last time religion came up in a conversation?"

What Has Been Your Experience . . .

The final phrase, of course, works the same way as the other four:

"What has been your experience with The Church of Jesus Christ of Latter-day Saints? *Who* do you know that attends our church, and *what* have they shared with you?"

"What has been your experience studying the life of Jesus Christ? *Where* did you obtain your knowledge of Jesus, and *what* effect has He had on your life?"

"What has been your experience with Latter-day Saint temples? *When's* the last time you saw one in your business travels, and *which* one was it?"

You may be asking yourself about now, *Do I have to always ask two questions following the relevant topic?* No, of course not. There are no hard-and-fast assessing rules when the Spirit is your guide. However, you will find that by asking two questions following the relevant topic, you will receive more substantive responses. And by doing it this way, you help the investigator feel that you're truly interested—not just checking a bunch of boxes on your "Questions to Ask Investigators Before Launching into a Lesson" form. It's almost like you have so much curiosity that you can't stop asking!

What if, though, the investigator doesn't actually answer the entire question you asked? For instance, you said, **"Share with us a little about your past experience with missionaries from our church; *how many* times did they visit you, and *what* do you remember most about the conversations?"** Instead of telling you "how many," they just go on about "what" they remember. Should you cut them off at some point and say, "Excuse me, Sir, you still haven't answered my question about 'how many' times they came!" Sure, if you like being tossed out of homes, do that!

Instead, I'm sure you'll see that the technique you're learning here is not designed to get every question answered that you ask, but to provide the investigator enough leeway to touch on or address that part of the topic that is most, well, *relevant* to them. That's why we use two Serving words and not just one. It simply doubles the chances of them finding something in your question that they want to address. (Of course, using more than two Serving words in one question is overkill, and you'll feel like an interrogator, not a teacher. So stay away from that.)

The point is, these are tools to help you in your role as an ambassador for Christ. He is interested in every one of His children. And you should be, too. This three-part technique helps you illustrate interest and concern in a thoughtful, conversational way.

The alternative to using this technique is to spin off rapid-fire questions that lead to one-word answers—if they even allow you to continue. That's not a dialogue, that's a survey.

Now, remember the back-and-forth earlier between the missionary and the farmer? I suggested that, among other things, one of its faults is that the missionary didn't follow up his relevant topic with any of the Serving words. Thus, the farmer was confused as to what the missionary wanted to know. That's when conversations end quickly.

Another reason it fell flat is that the missionary used "Dead-End Words":

1. Is
2. Was
3. Do
4. Does
5. Can
6. Could
7. Will
8. Would
9. Has
10. Have

While the intent behind these words—to learn more, of course—is good, the use of these words is not nearly as helpful as the Ten Serving Words. Why? Because they can easily lead to a yes or no answer. And then the missionary is still not sure what the investigator is thinking or the meaning behind their answer. Serving words, on the other hand, lead to substantive information.

In fact, it's impossible to use a Serving word in a question and get a yes/no answer. Try it! I'll bet you a milkshake on your P-Day that you can't. "Who?"—"Yes." "When?"—"No." See! Can't be done.

So, whenever you feel inclined to use a "Dead-End Word," stop yourself and use a Serving word instead. Helpful, insightful information will follow.

4. Conversation Starters

Now let's put some whipped cream on this sundae for you. Here is the final technique that, when used with relevant topics, Ten Serving Words, and Five Magical Phrases, will make assessing feel as natural as any conversation you've had with a friend back home. These conversation starters, as the name implies, come at the very beginning of each and any Magical Phrase:

1. **Just out of curiosity . . .**
2. **I'm curious . . .**
3. **If you could . . .**
4. **If you wouldn't mind . . .**
5. **I'm wondering . . .**

Here's how you might use them to make your assessing feel and sound more natural:

"Just out of curiosity, tell me about your business travel; where do you typically go, and how often are you able to attend a church service on the road?"

I don't know about you, but every time someone says "just out of curiosity," I feel as though they're asking this question for the first time, like they hadn't planned to ask but now their curiosity is just too great. Thus, I'm more inclined to want to answer.

And speaking of that:

"I'm curious; could you describe for me your views on life after death? Where do you think we go, and who do you think we'll meet when we get there?" Or:

"If you could, share with us your concerns about organized reli-gion. What might have happened in the past to sour you on it, and how much has that affected your views about God generally?"

"If you wouldn't mind, what do you think your parents would say if you told them you wanted to attend church with us? How might introducing them to our bishop help, and which of your parents would we speak with first?"

"I'm wondering, what has been your experience with addictions in your family? When did you first learn about them, and what kind of things are you teaching your kids so they can avoid them while they're young?"

I have taken each of the conversation starters here and matched them up with the Five Magical Phrases in the order you learned them. But you can mix and match all you want. It's not important that certain conversation starters go with certain Magical Phrases; it's just important that you try to lead every question with a softer opening that shows respect, consideration, and sensitivity to the topic you're about to explore.

When you use the conversation starters, investigators will recognize your thoughtfulness. They won't be offended by the question. They'll be appreciative of the way you ask—because every servant of the Lord assesses for understanding with care.

Limiting Your Questions

I've given you a *lot* of ways to effectively ask questions.

But don't go overboard. Remember that you're supposed to practice moderation so people don't think you're interrogating them (see *Preach My Gospel*, 184). If you don't do it tenderly, too much assessing and too many questions can confuse or distract your investigators from the purpose of your visit.

So, how can you limit the number of questions while making sure that you ask the most effective ones? Here is a reminder and some things to keep in mind.

We will not get upset if investigators don't answer all our questions exactly as we asked them. Let's imagine you ask, **"If you could, tell me about your family's experience going to church; what process did you use to select a church, and how long have you been attending?"** Now, say you get this long response: "Oh, you know, we struggled over which church to go to. My wife's Methodist. I'm Southern Baptist. Both our grandparents were raised Catholic. So, we've really struggled with the right denomination for our family. In fact, at times we've been divided, and we've actually gone separate directions on Sunday. But we've kind of decided that Lutheranism is probably a good middle ground for all of our beliefs."

Good stuff. But your investigator never did address how long they've been attending. No matter. Because he *did* share the process they went through in choosing a denomination. And that's something you're interested in learning because it seems to be of deep interest to him.

The specific questions and answers aren't as important as simply jump-starting an honest conversation. It's as though you're nudging them down the hill so they'll start sharing. Even if the first question doesn't yield the information you want, you can follow where they want to go—the area of most interest or greatest concern to them. *That's* what they probably want to talk about, and *that's* what will help you assess and understand. And if you initially asked a question about something that doesn't really matter to them, they'll forget you even asked—and that's fine.

Know that there's a difference between *learning questions*, which we do in assessing for understanding, and *teaching questions*, which we do as we're expounding doctrines, commandments, and principles. A *teaching question*—"What was the law of Moses and what were some of its tenets?"—can be heavy, intimidating, and fatiguing if not used well, especially if an investigator doesn't know the answer. In the early stages of the relationship, you want to stick to *learning questions*, questions that will help you learn more about your investigator.

Master your assessment skills by using questions in as many settings as you can. Here are some actual examples from missionaries in the field, taped during a training session I did with them—and, I hope, some helpful commentary from me:

"If you wouldn't mind, tell me about the education you've had; I mean, did you . . . where did you attend school, and how did that lead to a career?"

This started out to be a weak question, because it included "did you . . ." But the missionary caught himself. As you'll recall, *did* and *do* and *does* are all "Dead-End Words" (yes/no questions)—they close conversation instead of inviting expansion.

"If you could, give me an idea of your view on life after death; where do you think we go, and how do we make sure our family is there with us?"

This is a great series of questions, especially since the answers lead us gently into some core teaching principles.

"I'm curious; share with me the time you went into the army; why did you choose that particular branch of the military, and what did you gain most from the experience?"

That's a nice set of questions that will get someone talking.

"I'm wondering, what do you think about God? How has He influenced your family relationships, and why is it important to have God in your life?"

Notice that this missionary didn't ask, "What do you think about God? Is He important to you?" That could have invited a yes or no response. Instead, the missionary asked, "*How* is He important to you?" That invites a more thoughtful response, rich with context.

How do you ask questions in a way that doesn't sound pushy or invasive? Simple: first, be in tune with the Spirit. If you are, you'll know when to ask questions and how far to go in asking them. And as you practice and gain experience, your questions will sound more fluid, more articulate, more interested, more genuine.

Second, if you feel a desire to delve into a sensitive topic (family dynamics, health, marital status, contentious relationships, and so on) because the Spirit is suggesting it would be helpful to know more, *preface the question by stating its relevance.* In other words, before you ask the question, tell your investigator the *reason* you feel it's important to ask. Here's an example:

"We want to be helpful to you in this journey you're taking with God, and in order to do that, as His ordained ministers, it's always

helpful for us to understand a little better the family dynamics when we're teaching in a home. So, if you would, describe for us how your family unit came together; which of your children are with you full-time, and which of them spend time with their dad on weekends?"

With this brief explanation—prefacing the question by stating its relevance—the investigator hears that your purpose in asking is not to pry but to understand. They will appreciate your interest in them and your sensitivities as a missionary.

The Question to Avoid

By now, your head might be exploding from all the questions you could use when assessing an investigator.

So, I'll make this easy.

There's one question you should *never* ask when assessing.

It's the "Will you?" question. Here me out.

The "Will you?" question has become common throughout the Church. Elder V. Dallas Merrell, a former member of the Second Quorum of the Seventy, said, "We invite by asking a person, 'Will you?' To invite with 'Will you?' evokes a yes or no answer, which is an exercise of individual moral agency. Individual moral agency is at the heart of Heavenly Father's plan" ("Will You?" *Ensign*, October 2001).

Will you? is a powerful question to ask and will produce wonderful results—if used at the appropriate time. And that time is *not* when assessing. Why? Because it's a question that is used in "inviting," not in finding out information.

Missionaries correctly use the "Will you?" question when asking someone to make a commitment to the Lord, such as baptism. Those who are asked that question answer with a simple "yes" or "no."

Though this question isn't suited for assessing, do not underestimate its power when seeking commitments. As Elder Merrell said, "Although our personalities, gifts, and callings differ, our inviting will not fall on neutral ears, especially when prompted by the Spirit. For when we invite with 'Will you?' the Holy Ghost will testify of our invitation and encourage others to say yes" ("Will You?" *Ensign*, October 2001).

Avoid Becoming a "Sounding Brass"

You've read or heard the term *sounding brass*. What does it mean to avoid becoming "a sounding brass or a tinkling cymbal" (1 Corinthians 1:13)?

I believe it means simply going through the motions—void of charity, asking questions only to ask questions. Talking simply to hear yourself talk. Don't do it. Your message is too important to clutter it with thoughtless chatter. And your representation of the Lord is too significant to waste time—yours and that of others—with a bunch of hollow, meaningless questions.

A perfect example of a "sounding brass and tinkling cymbal" is a trivial question that's overused by just about everyone: "Would you be interested in . . . ?"

Think about it. What happens when people hear "would you be interested"? They put up their defenses. Why? Because this question proposes immediate commitment. And when someone is asked to make a commitment before he's ready, he will balk. He'll hesitate by saying something like *I dunno. Maybe. Sorta. Perhaps. It depends. Kinda. I'll see. Let me think about it.* Whatever happens, he won't say "yes," just in case there's some trick up your sleeve he can't detect yet. Then you're no further ahead than before. In fact, I'd say you've taken a step backward because you've leaped over the important "building trust" stage of the missionary/investigator relationship.

There's another reason you shouldn't use the question, "Would you be interested in?"—there are only two possible answers. One, of course, is "Yes." Okay, that's good. You'd like that. But it's also uncommon—meaning, you'll hear it only on rare occasions.

The other possible answer, and far more common, is "No." If people say, "No, I'm not interested," you're faced with either turning them around completely or showing them why they're wrong. Neither is a very encouraging task when you're trying to build a relationship of trust.

A better question to ask is, **"Have you ever considered . . . ?"**

Look at the difference. Instead of asking, "Would you be interested in coming to church with us this Sunday?" try, **"Have you ever considered attending or visiting a Latter-day Saint service?"** Both have only two possible answers—"yes" and "no"—but this way of asking gives you an option to continue the conversation.

Imagine the investigator says, "Yes, I've considered it, but I've decided against it." Is the conversation over? No. You have ample opportunity for follow-up questions: "How did you come to that decision?" "What happened in the past?" "Why do you feel that way?" The door is still open for further assessing. You're given the chance to listen more, assess further, and continue building trust.

If you ask the other way ("Would you be interested in coming to church with us this Sunday?") and get a "no," you've arrived at a dead end—and if you do try to ask more questions about it, you'll start to sound a bit pushy.

What happens if you get a "no" reply to "Have you ever considered . . . ?" as in, "No, I've never considered it"? Is the conversation over? Not by a long shot. After all, that doesn't mean, "No. I'm not interested." You now have a great opening to invite the investigator to church. She might say, "I've never given it any thought. Is it something I can do? I thought you had to be invited by a friend to go inside. Don't you need one of those little membership cards? That's what one of the guys at work told me about your church."

Just imagine where you can go from there!

A closely related "sounding brass and tinkling symbol" is the *if/then question.* Here's a common example: "If I could show you that there are living prophets on the earth today, then would you be interested in watching general conference with us this weekend?"

People are wary of if/then questions. And, again, they don't like the word "interested" because it sounds like you're seeking an immediate commitment from them.

But if you say, **"Have you ever *considered* the idea that there might still be prophets on the earth today, just like there were in the time of Christ?"** you have a good opening for further discussion regardless of whether they answer "yes" or "no."

To avoid "a sounding brass and tinkling cymbal," think before you speak. Are your questions really of merit? Are they really advancing the discussion? Are they really helping build trust and understanding? Or are they just your way of getting past the assessing process so you can get on with your prepared lesson?

Please pay special attention to Elder Jeffrey R. Holland's wonderful advice on how to assess for understanding:

> More important than speaking is listening. Ask these friends what matters most to *them*. What do *they* cherish, and what do *they* hold dear? And then listen. If the setting is right you might ask what their fears are, what they yearn for, or what they feel is missing in their lives. I promise you that *something* in what they say will *always* highlight a truth of the gospel about which you can bear testimony and about which you can then offer more. . . . If we listen with love, we won't need to wonder what to say. It will be given to us by the Spirit—and by our friends. ("Witnesses unto Me," *Ensign*, May 2001; emphasis in original)

If At First You Don't Succeed . . . , Pray and Practice

If you've applied yourself and tried to work through any of the assessing techniques I've described, you've probably discovered that assessing isn't always as easy as it may appear.

Don't be too tough on yourself. Remember: whenever you start to develop a skill, it's a bit awkward. It takes time and patience.

Maybe you're talented at playing the piano or baking a pie or shooting free throws. You can reasonably call it a skill because, while you took time to learn the technique originally, you can now do it without even thinking about it. You just do it. The same could be said about teaching skills.

At first, you might feel a bit uncomfortable or clumsy with the things you're learning in this book. But the more you practice, asking for the Lord's assistance, the faster those things become part of you. Before you know it, your conscious technique becomes your subconscious skill. And you achieve a smooth approach you can use with sincerity.

I remember the first day I began learning to drive a car as a fifteen-year-old. There were so many things to think about. I looked down and saw three pedals, but I only had two feet. How was *that* supposed to work? There was a little stick that came out of the console. It had a knob on top with a diagram showing how to put the car into gear (I assumed that's what it meant). But then I'm supposed to put my hand over the diagram to move the stick, preventing me from seeing the little drawing anymore. So, I have to take my hand off the stick to see how to put the car into gear, but I had to put my hand back on the stick to drive the car. I was toast.

That's just the beginning. I had to think about the radio and the air conditioner and the heater and wipers and blinkers and the mirrors I was supposed to constantly check. I had to obey all the rules of the road. I also had to watch out for pedestrians and other crazy drivers. Of course, I had to follow the directions to where we were going—all while my mom squirmed in the passenger seat and her fingernails dug into my arm.

No wonder learning to drive is so stressful. It's awkward. It's scary. And it's embarrassing—especially when stopped on a hill with a manual transmission! But guess what? I did it, and so, probably, did you. We both learned how to drive, and life went on. And now we don't even have to think about it—we just do it.

When it comes to developing teaching skills, you've got to do what you did when you learned to drive. You receive instruction. You practice repeatedly. And eventually it becomes a skill—part of your subconscious. So, if your performance is cumbersome at first, don't be concerned. Just keep praying and practicing.

***

A closing thought:

Members of our Church rightfully love to recount the wonderful lesson of "we will compare the word unto a seed," as told by Alma in Chapter 32 of the book that bears his name. But have you ever noticed that before he teaches this wonderful parable about faith, the first principle of the gospel, to the Zoramites, he actually asked them *five* questions? Then, after expounding the principle, he followed up with *six* more questions (see Alma 32).

Before he taught, Alma assessed for understanding. Then, when he was through, he assessed further to ensure *their* understanding of the principle. Why wouldn't today's missionaries want to do the same?

The ideas I've shared in this chapter are intended to assist you in considering your words and questions a little more thoughtfully. If you do, you'll get better answers, and those answers will supply inspiration. That inspiration will lead to greater teaching.

In the end, you can't baptize people you don't teach. And to teach, you must first understand, through assessing, those you are called to serve.

Chapter Seven

Skill 3: Presenting a Tailored Message

"Second only to the responsibility missionaries have to listen to the Spirit, is the responsibility they have to listen to the investigator. . . . If we'll listen with spiritual ears, . . . our investigators *will tell us* what lessons they need to hear!"

Elder Jeffrey R. Holland,
"The Divine Companionship," address given at the Seminar for New
Mission Presidents, June 26, 2009, emphasis in original.

Now that you've learned valuable and useful information about your investigator through assessing, should you dive in, head-first, with a message?

Not quite.

First you assess (which we just covered). Then you tailor what you're going to teach based on what you learned from the assessment (which we're going to talk about now). And then you teach with the Spirit as your guide (which we're also going to address in this chapter).

There are a few important things I'd recommend you do when you finish assessing:

1. **Thank your investigator.**
2. **Explain why you took the time to assess.**
3. **Show that you listened.**
4. **Demonstrate oneness with your companion.**

This isn't an involved ordeal. In fact, each of these steps requires no more than a sentence or two. Here's how I'd suggest doing it.

First, thank your investigator. Don't over-complicate it. Just be real. Say something like: **"Thank you for those insights."**

"Thank you for sharing with us some of your feelings about your family."

"Thank you for giving us a little background on your work situation. It was very helpful."

"Thank you for opening up to my companion and me so we know a little about your feelings toward religion."

"Thank you for your candor about scripture. We really appreciate your honesty."

Second, explain why you took the time to clarify those important topics or issues with them. You might say:

"The reason we wanted to learn these things is so we can tailor a message that is just right for your family." Or,

"We wanted to customize a lesson that we think addresses where you're at, and you've helped us do that tonight." Or,

"Because of the things you've shared with us, we're better able now to identify one of Christ's teachings that we believe speaks to your situation."

Here's the exciting thing about explaining why you took the time to assess: you're letting your investigator know that you didn't arrive with a stock presentation that's been prepackaged and memorized—one you're committed to deliver, no matter what they might say.

Or, here's another way to look at it: if you *don't* tailor your message and it *doesn't* have relevance to your investigator, he'll sit through it and politely nod and thank you for coming as he shows you the door. And after that, he might not answer your calls or your knocks. And you'll be wondering, as his phone goes to voicemail once again, *What happened?* But if your message has relevance to him, he will start to open up, letting the beauty of truth penetrate his heart and mind, inching him closer to conversion.

Third, show that you listened while you were assessing. Perhaps you'll say:

"Based on the things you've shared with us, and in our role as representatives of the Lord, may I suggest we discuss . . ." Or,

"And now, in the spirit of the same honesty you've demonstrated, we have a message we believe is suited to the challenges you're facing." Or,

"We'd like to offer something that would really apply to your family and the things going on in your life right now."

By saying something like this, you subtly yet strongly indicate a few things:

1. <u>You listened to them</u>. The sharing of their personal thoughts and feelings didn't fall on disinterested ears. You were paying attention.

2. <u>You listened to the Spirit</u>. ". . . based on our role as representatives of the Lord . . ." reminds them that you are there in His place. And as His messengers, you're entitled to know what He would have you say to them as His proxy. The Spirit is your third companion, whispering to you this guidance and direction.

3. What you're about to teach is <u>tailored specifically to your investigator</u>. Your message at this moment is based on what he shared with you about his personal needs, interests, achievements, and/ or concerns.

Fourth, and finally, demonstrate the oneness you share with your companion by asking, **"Elder (or Sister), would you agree that now would be a good time to discuss with Brother Frazer [what you will teach]?"** When your companion agrees, say something like, **"All right, let's continue."** Then begin your message.

Even after you go through these four brief steps, your investigator might request that you address another topic or principle. Go with it! Remain open and receptive to what the Spirit may indicate so you can address an investigator's curiosities or fears. And remember, just as you're entitled to the Spirit's help, so is your investigator. If he believes a certain topic might help him or his family—as taught by the Lord's servants—that is a manifestation of the Spirit working in his home and in his heart. Embrace it, commend him for it, and proceed with love and enthusiasm.

Elder Ronald A. Rasband has taught:

> The Holy Ghost . . . inspires, testifies, teaches, and prompts us. . . . We [including investigators] have the sacred responsibility to learn to recognize His influence in our lives and respond.
>
> My experience has been that the Spirit most often communicates as a feeling. You feel it in words that are familiar to you, that make sense to you. ("Let the Holy Spirit Guide," *Ensign*, May 2017)

The Spirit's participation at every stage of your engagement with an investigator is vital. When the Spirit tells you to press forward with your message, do it. When the Spirit impresses upon you that it's time to pivot and present a different thought, adjust. And if the Spirit tells you not to teach right now, that perhaps more or different preparation is needed before your teaching can be received, refrain (see D&C 42:12–14).

An Apostle's Principles of Teaching

Before we look at the details of proper presenting, I want to share a very powerful talk about teaching delivered by President Dallin H. Oaks in general conference (see "Gospel Teaching," *Ensign*, November 1999). Saying that there "are many different ways of teaching, but all good teaching is based on certain fundamental principles," he shared six principles of teaching. Allow me to add some brief thoughts regarding investigator teaching after each.

1. *The "teacher must have a love of God and others."* Below, I'll share a powerful example of how love works in teaching.
2. *"The teacher must be teaching for the good of others."* Our teaching must be done with the right intent. Your heart must be pure, and your motives must be appropriate. Your investigators and their needs should be your primary consideration whenever you teach.

3. *"We must teach from the prescribed material."* In other words, don't wander from the doctrine. Don't theorize. Don't dive into things that are speculative or inappropriate.
4. *"We prepare diligently."* Not only must you prepare a lesson with diligence, but every day you must diligently prepare to be a better missionary.
5. *"Teach as directed by the Spirit."* Be worthy of the Spirit, ask for the Spirit, and be receptive to the Spirit. Never ignore the Spirit's promptings or impressions.
6. *"Success is measured in results."* I love that President Oaks uses the word *results* as the sixth principle of good teaching. You will know you're an effective teacher based on the results your teaching provides in the lives of your investigators. And that's something you—and they—may not know or appreciate until days, weeks, months, or years later (if ever).

Love Precedes Proper Teaching

One reason the Apostle Paul was such an extraordinary missionary is that, despite his upsetting history of hate toward and persecution of the followers of Christ, he eventually repented and learned to love those he served. "O ye Corinthians, our mouth is open unto you, our heart is enlarged" (2 Corinthians 6:11). Though my example next to Paul's is like a grain of sand next to a boulder, let me share how developing love for people was essential before I could properly teach.

As I began my mission service in Japan, my ability to fully love the people was somewhat compromised because I was too judgmental of them. Don't get me wrong. I didn't judge what degree of heaven I thought they would obtain, but I did think, *That person would probably never accept the gospel message. We should probably spend our time elsewhere.*

That all changed the day I met Mr. Ikawa. The moment is so vivid in my memory that I can still recall the first time we knocked on his steel door on the eighth floor of a twenty-story apartment complex.

When Mr. Ikawa opened the door, I couldn't help but notice his tired, worn face. He couldn't have been older than thirty or so, but he looked like he was more than twice that age. It seemed apparent that he had experienced a tough life.

Despite our broken Japanese, he invited us to come out of the cold and into his tiny apartment. As we did, his wife scurried out with a baby in her arms and into what we thought was an adjoining room.

We learned that Mr. Ikawa was in the construction industry, which made sense—he was still in his work clothes, his hands and his face were dirty, and his hair was unkempt from the hardhat he must have been wearing all day. Despite this meek appearance, though, he became forceful when calling out to his wife, who cowered with her baby in what we later discovered was nothing more than a side closet. We didn't think to impose our values on him by asking if his wife could join us. Instead, we visited with him, but could hear her trying to keep the baby quiet in the very stark and chilly adjoining space.

The whole situation made me uncomfortable. After a few visits, I wrote the following in my journal: "We're teaching the gospel to this man while all the time his wife is sitting in a dark, closet-like room as her life goes by. When I think of that poor lady—wondering if she despises us coming, knowing that when we do it's time for her to crawl into her closet—I don't feel the joy of the Spirit. Are we contributing to this abusive behavior just by being here? Until the Lord changes His commandments of how to treat one's wife, I can't feel real good about Ikawa-san learning about and joining the Church."

Nevertheless, after each lesson, he would agree to our returning the next day. This continued for a number of visits.

Here's the point I want to make. If I had continued to look down on Mr. Ikawa and decided I couldn't teach in such an environment, I never would have experienced what would become some of the sweetest, most spiritual moments of my entire mission.

In that simple, plain apartment, Mr. Ikawa eventually learned the power of an eternal family and agreed to have his wife join us for discussions. The baby was even permitted to crawl around as we taught. I can distinctly recall to this day the smiles and laughter we all experienced at the Ikawa home as the love of Christ permeated that home and our interactions.

We are taught that we must become like "children" to enjoy the blessings of heaven (see 3 Nephi 11:37–38). I think the same must be said of missionary work. We must possess the humility and love of children in order to enjoy the full blessings of teaching Christ's gospel.

How grateful I am that we didn't judge Mr. Ikawa too harshly— that we were touched by the Spirit just enough to prompt us to return to this modest home and teach this well-meaning family. In doing so, my companion and I taught truths that I know brought light to a dreary apartment and that brought them closer to their Heavenly Father.

I don't know if the Ikawa family ever received baptism. I do know that I received many blessings by being able to teach them. And those blessings came about only because the Spirit led us and helped us to love this family—not because of what they had or how they looked, but because we knew that they, as children of a loving Father, deserved to know their worth and destiny as much as anyone else.

***

Presenting Your Message

Have you ever looked up an instructional video on YouTube, as I have, only to be more confused after watching it? What can be more frustrating than wanting to learn but not being able to understand the subject?

Let me share some wise counsel: "Before teaching the doctrines in the lesson, consider giving a simple overview of what you are going to teach. Help people see that it will have personal relevance for them" (*Preach My Gospel*, 177).

Why is a simple overview so important? Put yourself in the shoes of an investigator, who may know nothing about the principles and doctrines and Church history you teach. Now consider how frustrating it would be to have missionaries launch into a lesson if you don't know why it's relevant, where it's going, or what the intended outcome is.

Remember that what you're teaching is all new to your investigators. It's a new "language." As their gospel guardians, giving them a quick overview before the lesson begins provides assurance and prepares them for what's about to follow.

What you're doing in a discussion environment should never be a surprise or a secret to the people you teach. Always announce your purpose and communicate your intent, which is a necessary and appropriate part of creating an environment of trust.

As you teach, "Make sure that you ask enough questions and listen carefully to their answers so you have a firm understanding of how quickly and how well they are learning and applying the doctrines you are presenting" (*Preach My Gospel*, 180). Remember Alma teaching the Zoramites (see Alma 32)?

As you teach, you should pay careful attention to how your investigator prefers to learn.

How Do People Learn?

How do I best present a message? My quick answer: I don't know! Here's why: what you should say and how you should say it completely depends on the person you're teaching.

People just learn differently.

I have three grown sons, all of whom were very different in the way they learned as boys. How did I teach them a principle or discipline them or goof around with them? It was different with each one. Sure, there were some similarities, but most parents will agree that there's no one way to teach or discipline or entertain kids. Not only do they all learn differently, but they learn differently at each stage of their lives.

The same thing is true of the investigators you will teach.

Not only are people different, but the way that they like to learn is different as well. Some individuals prefer to learn by listening; they like to hear it. Others want to learn by observing; they need to see it. For them, sitting around and talking in a family room isn't good enough—they need to watch a video, look at a picture, or experience the principles in action. The latter group of people might need to see an example of how the Church operates or how members act in Christlike ways before they feel comfortable joining.

Some people simply need time to think about what they are learning. They need to ponder. The more they think about it, the more it begins to settle in their mind and in their heart.

Yet others prefer to learn by reading. These are the types of people who want to look at the fine print before making a major decision. They have to inspect the warranty, so to speak. You could talk to them all day, but because they don't prefer learning this way, you're unlikely to make progress with them. Instead, you should supply tools—such as a reading assignment—to help them.

Some people may not read well—something to be aware of and sensitive to. Years ago, I accompanied a member of our stake presidency on a ministering visit to a less-active member of the ward. During the visit, we challenged this good brother to take the prophet's challenge to read the Book of Mormon by the end of the year. I testified how taking the challenge had helped me.

After I testified, he finally leveled with us by saying, "I just don't like to read. I can't internalize things by reading them. It just doesn't work for me." He didn't say he had a learning disability, and I'm not suggesting that either. Maybe he did, but that's something I don't know.

As we started to talk about the Book of Mormon and some of the principles and doctrines it contains, I sensed that he needed to be encouraged to become more engaged in his study. Less passive and more active. He should be invited into group discussions and study sessions. It also became clear to me that he would learn better if he had an audio version of the Book of Mormon. When I asked him about that possibility, he said, "My wife got me the audio Book of

Mormon for Christmas a couple of years ago, but I've never even used it!"

I challenged him: "Don't read the Book of Mormon; *listen* to the Book of Mormon from now until the end of the year." I challenged him to listen to the audio book in his car every day on the way to work. "If you can do that," I promised, "you'll receive the same blessings that those of us who are reading the Book of Mormon are receiving."

Simply understanding that he had a different and preferred way of learning than I did helped me teach him more effectively.

***

Please be sympathetic to the many ways in which people learn. Find out your investigators' skills, personality, background, education, and anything else that would help you know how to effectively teach them. Because a tailored message doesn't merely describe the content of the message; it also describes the *way* in which the message is delivered to an investigator.

Methods to Match the Investigator

Let's look at a few examples of how teaching can be tailored to the individual by using different teaching methods.

Example 1: I was recently asked by a missionary how I would go about teaching the First Vision to one of his investigators. While tracting, he and his companion had come across a divorced mother of four. In assessing her situation, they learned she was struggling with her finances.

Imagine you're sitting in her simple living room with her four kids playing noisily around the house, and, based on your assessment of her situation and the Spirit's guidance, you conclude that it is best to teach this mother the story of the First Vision. How would you go about teaching in these circumstances? Here are some thoughts that may help her relate to and come to believe the story of Joseph Smith.

First, she has four children. Joseph Smith was young at the time of the First Vision, and he came from a large family whose members ended up supporting him through the difficult things that happened as the Church was restored. You might help this mother relate her relationship with and care of her children to the close family bonds that Joseph Smith and his family shared when he was younger.

Another idea would be to mention how Joseph came from humble circumstances. You could point out that despite—and maybe because of—his father's difficulty in providing for the family, Joseph was in a position, spiritually, to receive God's word.

Because of her unfortunate circumstances, this investigator is probably desperate for a positive change, but she may be uncertain how to restore happiness in her life. You might share how Joseph Smith was also looking for a change in his life—looking for truths that would help. He wondered how so many seemingly well-intentioned people had such conflicting opinions and gave him such different advice. You might point out that Joseph wanted to know how to be happy, so he finally decided he needed to go to the scriptures and God as the best sources for truth and guidance.

Perhaps using one of these approaches would help you adapt your teaching style to this mother's needs so she connects better with the message.

Example 2: Let's consider another simple scenario. Suppose you're teaching an antsy seven-year-old boy whose father is a member of the Church but whose mother is not. They've agreed to let the boy be taught because he's going to be turning eight soon, and the dad thinks it would be special if he could be baptized on his eighth birthday.

The father has placed his trust in you—yet how are you going to relate to this seven-year-old boy? If you have an animated Joseph Smith video, you might ask him about the kind of cartoons he watches or video games he plays. Then ask if he'd like to watch a cartoon about one of your favorite people in the whole world: Joseph Smith. You could show him the part about the First Vision and talk about it as you watch together.

Or you could ask him about his favorite outdoor activities, then explain—or, better yet, demonstrate—Joseph's favorite game of pulling sticks. If he has chores his parents ask him to do, you could explain how Joseph Smith lived on a farm and had lots of chores to do.

You might ask if this young boy likes to read and what his favorite books are. Then tell him that Joseph liked to read, too, and one of his favorite books was the family Bible. You could share the pivotal verse Joseph read in the Bible (see James 1:5) and what happened as a result (see Joseph Smith—History 1:11–20).

Or maybe there have been times at school when the boy didn't know the answer to a question. You can relate how Joseph Smith didn't know the answer to a question, and you can explain what he did about it (see Joseph Smith—History 1:10–20). This might also be a great way to teach him how to pray and that faith leads to answered prayers, even for small boys.

These are only a few examples of how your teaching should be tailored to the individual. As we are encouraged in the Introduction to *Preach My Gospel*, "You can teach the lesson in many ways" (*Preach My Gospel*, viii). A humble teacher is prepared to alter teaching methods and examples depending on the investigator's present situation, background, and level of understanding.

Before we had the resource *Teaching in the Savior's Way*, the book *Teaching, No Greater Call: A Resource Guide for Gospel Teaching* (1999) presented nearly twenty-five pages of different teaching methods. It suggested lots of ways to teach: dramatizations, brainstorming, case studies, role playing, even puppets. If you find it difficult as a missionary to know which of the various teaching methods to incorporate in your discussions, you might locate this resource guide and carefully review the helpful suggestions it contains.

Studying and practicing different teaching methods may be a great way to spend companion study time. Then try them with the people you're teaching. When you exercise faith, show obedience, and try to improve your teaching skills, the Lord will help.

Conclude with a Commitment Question

"Commitment is an essential part of repentance," teaches *Preach My Gospel.* "It is the act of obligating oneself to a course of action and then diligently following through on that decision" (*Preach My Gospel,* 197).

Elder Jeffrey R. Holland taught: "When you teach [people] to keep their commitments, you are teaching them to become covenant-keepers" ("Making and Keeping Covenants," Missionary Satellite Broadcast, April 25, 1997; *Preach My Gospel,* 198).

Some missionaries may feel uncomfortable asking an investigator to make a commitment. But in fact, you're serving that person by training them that commitments made with you are actually promises made to God. "Keeping promises," taught Elder Ronald A. Rasband, "is not a habit; it is a characteristic of being a disciple of Jesus Christ" ("Standing By Our Promises and Covenants," *Ensign,* November 2019). As they are learning the gospel, commitments are practice for entry onto His covenant path. If they can learn that pattern as an investigator, they will be a stronger and more converted member of the Church of Jesus Christ.

Therefore, after you teach a principle, ask your investigator to commit to do something related to that principle. (A commitment could be anything from reading a chapter of scripture or praying as a family to attending a church meeting or being baptized.) This is the "Will you?" question I talked about in Chapter Six, and now is the perfect time to use it (see *Preach My Gospel,* 199).

Here's another way of going about it:

"Based on what we've shared with you today–based on the lesson that we've just covered; based on this principle we've shared with you; based on these scriptures we've read together–is there anything that would *keep you from* praying with your family this evening?" Or,

"Is there anything that *keeps you from* visiting us on Tuesday night and letting us show you around the church?" Or,

"Is there anything that *keeps you from* attending sacrament meeting this Sunday and sitting with our ward mission leader?"

Ask direct questions. (Examples of some helpful direct questions to obtain a commitment are listed in *Preach My Gospel*, 197.)

You might say, **"Will you read in third Nephi . . . ?"** Or,

"Will you pray and ask Heavenly Father?" Or,

"Will you attend church this Sunday and allow us to have a member pick you up?" Or,

"Will you begin now to abstain from alcohol for the next twenty-four hours?" Or,

"Will you invite your husband to meet with us?"

It could even be something as simple as, **"Will you permit us to come to your home tomorrow night and continue this discussion?"**

There are two possible answers to the commitment question: yes or no. You want a *yes*. If you hear it, you're set. Confirm with the investigator his or her commitment and what will follow.

What if you get a *no*? You now know the investigator has concerns. In that case, you should listen and resolve the concerns—the skill we'll cover in the next chapter.

As you present a tailored message, you are acting in the Lord's stead to teach His children. What power. What responsibility. And what a blessing it will be in your life to know that you were a worthy spokesperson for Jesus Christ.

> But a commandment I give unto you, that ye shall declare whatsoever thing ye declare in my name, in solemnity of heart, in the spirit of meekness, in all things.
>
> And I give unto you this promise, that inasmuch as ye do this the Holy Ghost shall be shed forth in bearing record unto all things whatsoever ye shall say. (D&C 100:7–8)

Chapter Eight

Skill 4: Proper Listening to Resolve Concerns

"God's children should learn to listen, then listen to learn."

President Russell M. Nelson,
"Listen to Learn," *Ensign*, May 1991

You're a communicator.

Like it or not, try or not try, you communicate through reading, writing, speaking, body language, and mostly listening. It's a daily activity.

And though our parents and teachers spent countless hours teaching us to read, write, and speak, interestingly—and regretfully—few of us have ever been trained how to listen. But our prophet implores all of us to aspire to become better.

If you're like most, you probably haven't thought a lot about listening.

Well, now's the time to do it. As a missionary for The Church of Jesus Christ of Latter-day Saints, you have a responsibility to not just *talk to* God's children, but to *listen to them* as well. "Wherefore, my beloved brethren, let every man be swift to hear, slow to speak . . ." (James 1:19).

Day-to-day, how will you listen to your companion? To your mission president during an interview? To the mission mom when she's speaking? To an investigator? To your ward missionaries? To the calls with family members back home?

This chapter is about helping you understand how you listen today and how you should listen moving forward. It will also point out some other approaches to resolving people's concerns that could prove beneficial, especially in your work as a missionary.

Listening isn't as simple as you might assume; actually, it's part art and part science. In his book *Seven Habits of Highly Effective People*, the late Dr. Stephen R. Covey, a former Brigham Young University professor and world-renowned author and lecturer, identified five ways of listening:

1. **Pretend listening**
2. **Passive listening**
3. **Selective listening**
4. **Attentive listening**
5. **Empathic listening**

For our purposes here, I'll attempt to simplify Dr. Covey's definition of each, and I invite you to consider which seems most similar to your own style or habits today.

Pretend Listening

This one's quick and easy to define: you're quiet while the other person is speaking, but your mind is somewhere else. Totally. You don't even respond, mostly because you haven't really heard anything that was said. You might know it as *daydreaming*. If you daydream while someone is talking to you, you're a pretend listener. It's not an effective form of listening, and it can damage relationships, not to mention reputations.

Passive Listening

In passive listening, you hear just enough to respond. Sort of.

It's a lot like distraction. You're "listening," but you're mostly thinking about something else you have to do, a run-in you had with an investigator, some things you need to remember to tell the mission president tonight, or how much that person across the room looks like Uncle Ross back home.

Passive listening happens when you're with other people but doing something else—like watching television, reading, surfing the internet, staring at your phone, or playing a video game. The usual response during passive listening is, "Uh-huh."

Have you ever been introduced to someone then forgotten their name in the next nanosecond? That's usually a sign of passive listening. It means that you heard enough to respond—with something harmless, such as, "Good to meet you"—but your mind was really somewhere else.

I've got a great—actually, terrible—example. My sons and I were watching a thrilling game on TV. My wife, Allison, strolled into the room and asked me, "Rob, have I gained weight?"

Focused on the game and not on what Allison said, I replied, "Where?"

Let's just say that was not a good answer. I'll spare you the details of what happened next. (In my defense, I thought she said, "Should we get steak?" At least I'm sticking to that.)

Whenever you listen to anyone in any situation, "Be sure to give people time to complete their thoughts before you respond, and do not interrupt while they are talking" (*Preach My Gospel*, 187).

Selective Listening

With selective listening, you hear what you want to hear.

We are taught, "While others talk to you, avoid the tendency to think about what you are going to say. Make sure you are really concentrating on the person speaking rather than planning your response" (*Preach My Gospel*, 185).

A selective listener hears only what he wants to hear because he can't wait to get his two cents in. He's thinking, *I see where he's going with this.* He's watching for the other person to take a breath so he can hurry and interject. Selective listeners listen to respond. They think, *When is she going to be quiet so I can talk?* instead of thinking, *What else can I do to understand her and to demonstrate that I understand?*

I don't think Abinadi was a selective listener. I don't think Ammon was, either. In fact, when you read their stories in the Book of Mormon, notice that they allowed wicked kings or priests to say whatever was on their minds—to state their case—before responding.

Attentive Listening

Most of us learned attentive listening in grade school.

You remember: your teacher said, while snapping her fingers, "Hello, class, pay attention! Eyes up here! I want your undivided attention."

As a result, you—and everybody else—grew up thinking that the best way to listen was to give someone your undivided attention.

A story in *Preach My Gospel* about the Sanchez family provides a great example of how a missionary used attentive listening:

> My companion and I were teaching the Sanchez family. It was hot and the children were making a lot of noise. I asked Sister Sanchez about her reading the Book of Mormon. As she began to explain, I noticed that their son had grabbed my companion's notebook and was running around the room waving it in the air. Although I was looking at Sister Sanchez, my mind was elsewhere. I thought to myself, "It's so hot, and I wish their little boy would settle down. This just isn't going to work." As my mind wandered, I noticed Sister Sanchez was struggling to talk. A subtle impression came into my mind to listen. I fought to tune out the heat and the noise. I carefully watched her face as she spoke. She looked down at the ground, then back up at my companion and me. Her husband was hopelessly trying to quiet the children. There was a pause, and then with trembling in her voice she said, "I did what you asked. I read those chapters you wanted me to, and I prayed." Again she paused and looked down. She glanced at her children, then her eyes met mine. "I got an answer," she said with a smile and with tear-filled eyes. "It's true, I know it's true." The Spirit filled the room. With

a heart full of gratitude that I had listened, I smiled and said, "Yes, it is." (*Preach My Gospel*, 187–188)

Only after this missionary used his best attentive listening skills did great things happen in that discussion, allowing the Spirit to touch all who were present.

Empathic Listening

The optimum form of listening, as taught by Dr. Covey, is empathic listening. Not *emphatic*. Not *pathetic*. The term *empathic listening* comes from the word *empathy*.

With empathic listening, **you listen to understand before you respond**. In other words, you must understand a problem or concern before you can solve it.

We are taught, "When you listen carefully to others, you understand them better. When they know that their thoughts and feelings are important to you, they are more likely to be receptive to your teachings, share personal experiences, and make commitments. As you listen, you will be able to more effectively adapt your teaching to their needs and interests" (*Preach My Gospel*, 187).

Empathic listening is *not* listening to agree. For example, you should never agree with someone's concern about or objection to the gospel. When someone says, "Oh, man, I have to *give up smoking*?" I would never recommend that you respond, "I've got to admit that's kind of a tall order. Why don't we skip that one?"

You should *listen to* a concern, but you should never *agree with* a concern. Don't get me wrong, I'm not advocating for contention. This isn't your cue to start debating an investigator on why she's wrong and you or the Church is right. What I am saying is that as soon as you agree with a person's concern, you validate it. You just gave her permission to own that concern. You essentially gave her an excuse not to make commitments to Christ or receive baptism.

Here are two other reasons we, as missionaries of Christ, should not agree with the objections we hear:

1. Most objections are simply opinions. When someone says, "Two hours on Sunday seems like a lot of time to spend at church," that's an opinion. When he claims accepting a calling is burdensome and ties him up, that's an opinion. Or if she claims that commandments tie us down, that's an opinion once again.

Why agree with an opinion that is contrary to the will of the Lord? Why agree with a point of view that differs from others who find great blessings in two-hour church or magnifying callings or obeying the commandments?

2. Many objections are actually not a commentary on the Church or its teachings as much as they are a reflection of the person stating them. Therefore, why agree with it?

For instance, if I claim that the Word of Wisdom is too stringent, couldn't that be more a reflection on me—my lack of faith, or my lack of self-control, or potential selfishness more than a regard for family members who have to deal with my potential addiction? Why, as a representative of the Lord and His Church, would you want to agree with someone whose personal choices prevent him from obeying a commandment?

Again, our purpose here is not to suggest that an investigator's concern means it's open season for proving him wrong. It's to encourage you to be an empathic listener. How do you do that? By listening to understand before you respond.

Let's put it this way: Instead of agreeing *with* the concern, be agreeable *to* the concern. There's a difference between agreeing with a concern and being agreeable toward the person expressing the concern. An agreeable missionary isn't combative or confrontational. An agreeable missionary is helpful, optimistic, and open. The missionary wants to listen and understand the concern. *Then* the missionary resolves it.

It's worth noting here that no matter your calling or experience or good intentions, it's extremely difficult to resolve a concern that you don't understand. Oh, you can try, of course! But to solve what you believe to be a concern of an investigator when it isn't, is a ticket to

Nowheresville. It's like trying to feed a toddler that isn't hungry anymore. They get angry and you grow frustrated. To avoid this uncomfortable dynamic with an investigator, first understand the investigator's concern. Then resolving it is welcomed and appreciated.

Because in the end, all people really want is to be understood. More than being right, more than winning an argument, your investigators—your companion, your neighbor, your ward mission leader—just want to be understood. And when they're not, friction follows.

Have you ever said this about a supervisor or roommate or ex-boyfriend: "They just don't understand." Or, "They just don't get it." See? Lack of understanding. And when that exists, relationships are harmed and sometimes severed. As representatives of Christ's Church, we can't ever be accused of not trying to understand another's point of view.

Elder Quentin L. Cook put it simply when, at the conclusion of his speech in June 2019 to the semiannual Jewish-Latter-day Saint Dialogue event at the BYU Jerusalem Center in Israel, he said, ". . . we join together to seek understanding and build respect between our two communities. It is a time to listen to one another and learn from one another."

What do you do, as an effective teacher, to truly understand a concern? You clarify. You ask questions. Since there's no such thing as a mind reader, don't *assume* you know what someone means, especially when topics are as sensitive as one's personal religiosity and relationship to God.

Here's another example of why to clarify (the "how to" is coming shortly). Maybe in the ward or branch where you serve, there are members who won't give you any referrals. You might have all kinds of ideas about why that is. But if you talk to them and use empathic listening, you'll find out they're not giving you referrals for a reason. You'll discover that they have a concern. They have a fear or an issue. You might find out that the last missionary they gave a referral to embarrassed them in front of their friends or family. Once you understand that, you can do something about it.

As an empathic listener, you listen fully to what someone has to say. You're not sitting there thinking, *I can't wait for him to stop talking so I can get to this point I want to make.* Or, *I've got a zinger for that objection. Just wait until she hears this one!* Or maybe, *Yeah, yeah, I've heard that a hundred times. C'mon, wrap it up so I can get to my next question.*

There's a real disconnect in thinking that way (besides the obvious one of being unsympathetic) because empathic listeners never think ahead. They don't have an agenda, either strategically or figuratively. They listen to understand, and their careful listening will tell them what to ask or clarify next.

As suggested earlier, a lack of understanding is what causes relationships to break up—socially, professionally, and diplomatically. People end relationships because of a lack of understanding between them, not because one person is always right and the other is always wrong. Wars start because of a lack of understanding between nations. "You don't understand our history . . . our culture . . . our religion . . . our values!"

How does this apply to missionary work? Your investigators don't need to be right. They need to be understood. And you're the one who can provide that understanding through empathic listening.

Guess why people don't invite the missionaries back after what seemed like such a good discussion? Guess why they won't answer the door anymore after a pleasant conversation at that same door two days earlier? Because they don't feel understood. More specifically, they don't feel that their concerns have been understood. They believe the missionaries aren't truly interested in what they think, they're more interested in their own objectives or ambitions.

As you listen to understand, not only to the person who is speaking but also to the Spirit, you are ready to step into that discussion and be guided by the Spirit in response to what the investigator shares with you. And because you're well prepared and well versed in the scriptures, the Spirit can whisper to you which teaching should come out of your mouth. What a gift!

President Russell M. Nelson said:

Let your response be warm and joyful. And let your response be relevant to that individual. Remember, he or she is also a child of God, that very God who dearly wants that person to qualify for eternal life and return to Him one day. You may be the very one to open the door to his or her salvation and understanding of the doctrine of Christ. ("Be Thou an Example of the Believers," *Ensign*, November 2010)

This kind of listening requires the kind of love that Jesus showed: "He loved them unto the end" (John 13:1). Always pray for love and an appreciation for everyone you teach and encounter—and a desire to understand them as much as to teach them.

How to Clarify: Uncovering True Concerns

Exercising empathic listening skills will help you be successful in resolving a person's concerns. So how do you do it? The first step is to understand the difference between true concerns and false concerns, which I sometimes call "decoy" concerns.

Most concerns (or objections) are false concerns—the tip of the iceberg, a metaphor referred to on pages 188–189 in *Preach My Gospel*. The iceberg metaphor suggests that when someone describes an issue they're having, most of the time it's not the real issue. The true concern is beneath the surface. People don't do it maliciously or to be dishonest. They do it because they're either not trusting yet, or they're uncomfortable sharing their true concern.

Why?

There can be a few reasons.

First, it's easier to come up with a concern that points the finger at someone or something else instead of admitting one's own true concern. You've probably heard these before: "My husband wouldn't want to hear your message," or, "Your church is too restrictive," or, "You people don't like to have any fun." Protecting yourself by blaming others for your fears is a defense mechanism that doesn't require self-examination.

Another reason for false concerns is that people don't think you love them enough or are interested enough in them to entrust you with their true concern. Instead, they give you a decoy concern. They say, "You know what? I like to go boating on Sunday. I don't think I can go to church." Or, "I'm just too busy at work." Those are false concerns and not the real issues preventing them from making life-improving decisions.

Easy for you to say, you might be thinking. *How do I figure out what's false and what's not?*

Good question.

Let's offer some suggestions.

There are several ways to clarify whether a concern is true or false when you first hear it. One way is to *restate it in your own words*—then stand back and watch an amazing thing happen as a result. Imagine someone says to you, "You know, my grandfather was LDS, but he had a disagreement with the Church back then. So, our family hasn't been back ever since. That was twenty-five years ago, and that's why I'm not a member of the Church."

Okay. Before you restate that concern in your own words, it's smart to ask them to elaborate—to tell you more. Because if you try to resolve the first thing they say, you might be addressing the wrong concern (a false concern). Tip: it's nearly impossible to resolve a false concern, because once you think you have, there's always another issue.

So, back to the example. You just heard this gentleman claim that his lack of desire to join us began with an episode his grandfather had with the Church. Don't repeat *exactly* what the investigator said to you. For one thing, you'll sound like a parrot. For another, it's possible he'll feel no need to elaborate. And you know what that means: you'll stay perched on the tip of the iceberg. You and the false concern.

You *can* get someone to elaborate by restating with a slight twist. I don't mean to say you should twist his words, but I do find that if you repeat his concern as you heard it—without using the exact words he did—he'll likely expound further on the concern. Why is that? You know the answer. Say it with me now: "Because people want to be understood."

Here's how you'd do that in the example of the offended grandfather: **"Your grandfather had a disagreement with a doctrine of the Church, and ever since then your family hasn't wanted to return?"**

Your investigator will say, "No, no, that's not what I said. What I, . . . no. It has nothing to do with the doctrine."

Did you catch the important clue he just gave? Listen as he elaborates: "No, no, it wasn't the doctrine. It was, uh, it was his bishop at that time. That guy was really heavy-handed."

Now, you wouldn't want to leave it at that, of course. Not that we want to dig up old graves, but you'd probably need to drill down further. Go ahead and tap the assessing techniques you learned in Chapter Six. (**"If you wouldn't mind, could you tell me a little bit about what happened; how the conflict began, and what impact it had on your family?"**) As you drill down and gain more information, you'll be better qualified to resolve the concern. But let's not get ahead of ourselves.

Another, complementary way to clarify a concern is to *ask probing questions* (that cannot be answered with "yes" or "no") with the same assessing techniques. For example, you might say, **"I'm curious, describe for us your grandfather's situation at the time; how long had he been attending church, and how did he and the bishop try to resolve the matter?"**

Now your investigator will give you a little more information: "Oh, he was devout all his life, practically. But he was so upset about a calling he was given that he never talked to the bishop or anyone else from the ward again."

Not to minimize in any way the seriousness of people's concerns, but the approach you should use is pretty clear: *Care and listen to what someone is saying, and you'll know what to ask next.* Remember that you're trying to help people articulate their own concerns. You're trying to drill down to the true concern. You're not toying with people or being deceptive in intentionally stating their concerns inaccurately. If you believe you know what someone's true concern is, you should state it and seek confirmation right away—but that's more the exception than the rule.

Now, let's see how all this works. Here is an exchange that might take place after you've just presented an investigator with a gospel principle. He then says, "I appreciate what you're saying, and I think you make a lot of sense. But I don't feel right meeting with ministers at this point in my life. I don't think we should continue, unless those ministers really know what they're doing and are well-trained and all. So, I'm really not interested in participating in your church. No offense, you seem like nice young men, but . . . well, thanks for coming. And by the way, nice tie." He then invites his wife to escort you and your companion to the door as he reaches for the remote.

You would be justified if your first thought is that the investigator doesn't want to be around ministers. But that's a false concern. How are you going to figure that out—and drill down to the real concern? Remember: you can either restate the concern or ask a probing question (or both).

Here goes: you respond by restating (somewhat), **"So, Brother Leavitt, you've lost interest in meeting with ministers unless they're a certain age?"**

Now listen carefully to what the investigator says next: "No, it has nothing to do with their age. In fact, I think it's great you two are devoting your time right now to this. You seem like you're doing it for the right reasons. But I don't think, after the experiences I've had, I want to get into it with ministers anymore."

Listen carefully to what he just said.

Let's try a probing question: **"If you wouldn't mind, tell me about your experiences with ministers."** (Notice in this case I'm not necessarily following up with two of the Serving words. In this delicate moment, I want to pull back and let him do as much of the talking as possible.)

Again, listen intently to the investigator's reply: "I don't wanna get it into it now, but . . . , yeah, it was an experience all right! And I didn't appreciate it. And my family wasn't too happy, either. I just think that when you go to church it ought to be a good experience.

It shouldn't be something that causes contention between you and the guy up at the front. I mean, if I want hellfire and damnation, I'll turn on the late-night cable shows and get it there, you know what I mean? I don't need that, especially if I'm skipping the game to go to church."

You now try to clarify (maybe it's a faith issue?): **"So what you're saying is that you've lost some faith because you have a hard time trusting people in the ministry?"**

The investigator continues, "Um, well, I've never really thought about this as a faith issue. I mean, it could be, but I've never really thought about it that way. I just can't really trust clergy who are getting paid to preach a popular message with a certain style—you know what I mean? Because then it's just a big show every Sunday to see who can put on the best sermon and win the biggest audience to bring more people into their church. That's what it seems like to me, especially based on my experience a few months ago."

Now you're getting somewhere. You're approaching the true concern. Keep drilling down, patiently, by asking another probing question—this one getting to the core of the issue: **"If you wouldn't mind, what was the experience you had a couple months ago?"**

The investigator then offers it up: "Well, I didn't really want to get into this right now (he turns off the TV), but we went to church after being away for several months. We sat close to the front, which I hate, but my wife kind of pulled us up there. I was feeling pretty good about myself for getting out of the house on Sunday. In fact, my wife was surprised that I wore a buttoned-down shirt. Then the minister started talking about people in my type of profession and how they're sinners. Right in front of my grandkids! I mean, no sensitivity whatsoever. He stood there slamming on people in my line of work. I think he was using an example of something he had experienced that week, and just decided we're all bad guys!"

You keep listening. You don't interrupt. You don't rush. Seeing your sincere interest, the investigator continues, "And then I had to address this issue with the grandkids after we got home. You know what that's like? They're asking me questions they shouldn't be asking their papa, thinking that I'm dishonest just because of how I make a living. It's an honorable profession. It's certainly put food on our table. I found the minister's story insulting. He had no sensitivity at all. I don't even know where he comes up with this stuff. How do you trust a guy like that?"

You can sense that you're getting closer to the real concern. As this point, you ask, **"I'm curious, Brother Leavitt, how do you think a minister should select and deliver a message to his congregation?"**

He says, "Well, I'd like a minister to make me feel good about coming to church. I like uplifting sermons. Right? I mean, who doesn't need to be motivated every once in a while? I'd like some encouragement from clergy."

You silently thank the Lord for His help in understanding this good man! The investigator has given you a window into his true concern. Remember what the false concern was: not interested in meeting with untrained ministers.

Your next step is to understand what would help resolve this concern. You might ask, **"What has been your experience when you've heard a great sermon? How does it make you feel, and what impact does it have on your day?"**

"Well, hmm. I guess in the end, it gives me hope. And it doesn't make me feel like a stranger—like I'm out of place and don't really belong. If I'm going to go, I want to have a good feeling. I want to walk out with a smile, not with a chip on my shoulder. That's not the kind of environment I want to be in if I make the effort to go to church."

You might continue, **"And, tell me, what effect would that kind of sermon have on your family?"**

He looks at his wife. "It would make us happy to be there. We'd be able to forget about the world for an hour or so and think about things that are . . . gee, I can't believe I'm saying this in front of my wife . . . things that are a little bit bigger than my job." He smiles. "Bigger than the football game I'm missing right now. If I could find a minister who does that, who encourages me and encourages my family, it'd be easy to go to church."

Okay. Based on what you've heard, what's the true concern(s) of this investigator? He told you he wants church to bring him and his family encouragement and hope. And along the way, he doesn't want to be belittled. He doesn't want to feel small. That's it.

Now you're uncovering the true concerns and understanding what would motivate him to come. Because you demonstrated sincere interest, restated, and probed, you learned that his initial statement—"I don't want to be around untrained ministers"—wasn't what was keeping him from going to church. You've learned that he wants to go to a place where he feels kinship with his minister, where there's mutual respect, and where there's a relationship that will serve him and his family well.

Let's look at some ways that same discussion could have gone wrong. Spoiler alert: they involve argumentation or debate.

What would have happened if you had taken his original statement—his false concern—at face value and responded by telling him that our Church doesn't have a paid ministry? He might have thought, *You're not really listening, because that has nothing to do with my concern.* Then, after an awkward pause, he'd say, "Well, good for you. Thanks for coming. You're nice guys. I hope you enjoyed the sandwich. Honey, would you please see these gentlemen to the door—and have you seen the remote?"

Or you could have answered, "Our minister is actually called the bishop. And the calling of a bishop is mentioned in the Bible. Would you like to see that reference? Let's open the New Testament together."

That wouldn't have gone any better. The investigator would have thought, *Okay, you're not listening. Thank you very much.* And he might have said, "That's nice. Now if you'll excuse me, the game's about to start."

You'll notice in the proper example we reviewed, the missionary didn't defend himself or the Church's way of doing things. He didn't debate. And thank goodness, the missionary didn't say, "Don't you think you're being a little too sensitive?"

Because the missionary refrained from argumentative or condescending tones, the investigator could sense and hear and see that the missionary was an empathic listener (though he probably wouldn't know that term). And because of that, the investigator was willing to give more information, piece by piece. The Spirit may have even whispered to him that the missionary, as a representative of the Lord, was truly interested in understanding. That's when an investigator will elaborate. That's when trust grows. And love is present.

Two Types of True Concerns: Public and Private

When it comes to true concerns, there are really two kinds: public and private. People don't mind divulging public concerns, but usually find it difficult to share private concerns.

Public concerns are those issues or objections that people comfortably believe "everyone" has, or those objections that you or the Church hear a lot. In other words, it's not just them. Here's an example: "I can't join your church because I grew up in a Catholic family, and it would be hard to break tradition."

At times, public concerns can be excuses, an easy "out." The investigator may think, *There's no way they'll have a good answer for this one*, so the investigator just tosses something out that may or may not be sincere. You know, though, that whatever he says, it's always time to clarify, as we've discussed.

On the other hand, often, underneath the public concern, a very private concern lurks, which for her is the real reason she hesitates or doesn't want to commit. For the individual above who claimed she didn't want to break with family tradition, the private concern may be: "My relationship with my parents is already strained because they don't like my boyfriend. If they heard I was meeting with the Mormon missionaries, too, they'd freak! They'd *never* come visit to meet Nigel."

Or, another private concern I heard once was, "We've moved around a lot, and our kids are just starting to make new friends in this neighborhood. One of the families here has already invited us to their church, and I'm afraid if we attended yours, we might lose them as friends—which could devastate our kids."

The bottom line? Even after your best efforts to clarify and uncover the true concern, sometimes it won't happen. The true concern is very private or personal. Don't take it personally. It doesn't mean you aren't worthy of hearing it or the investigator wouldn't want to share it, but on occasion the private concern is just that—private— and "now isn't the time."

That's why you need to rely on the Spirit to direct you what to say or do next. When to probe further or when not to. When to let it go or when to press ahead.

Common Concerns

If you want to understand people, try to put yourself in their shoes. This is why we trust the Savior—He understands us because He has walked every troubling, scary, temptation-laden path. He overcame them all. "To him that overcometh will I grant to sit with me in my throne, even as I also overcame, and am set down with my Father in his throne" (Revelation 3:21).

Part of being Christ-like is trying to see what others see from their point of view. It doesn't mean we have to live their life or make some of the bad choices found in the world, but it helps to have a basic understanding of the common concerns that keep people from making commitments to Christ. Do any of these sound familiar?

1. **Fear.** Fear of change or fear of the unknown. It takes courage to consider change and to make commitments that could lead to a new way of living.
2. **Demanding schedule.** Many people will say they're too busy to think about church or spiritual things that don't have practical meaning in their daily life, especially with other pressing priorities and deadlines weighing on them.
3. **Family rejection.** "They'll laugh; they'll ridicule me!" "They might cut me out of their will." "They'll refuse to babysit my kids; in fact, they might not even let my kids play with cousins." "They'll disown me."

4. **Loss of friends.** "My kids are in competitive sports and those families have become our circle of friends; now you're telling me we can't play on Sundays anymore? We'd not only be taking away the one thing that builds up my daughter's self-esteem, but we could lose a lot of our friends this way."

5. **"Anti-Mormon" sentiment.** With the proliferation of information—more than we can ever absorb, whether factual or not—anyone's theory or rumor can become someone else's basis for not adhering to the tenants of Christ's Church.

6. **Commitment avoidance.** Some people simply don't like commitment—of any kind. They may feel commitment means a loss of freedom.

7. **Apathy.** Apathy toward religion or spiritual devotion holds people back from progressing. *What's the use of trying?*

8. **The Sunday issue.** "Boy, you guys are at church forever, aren't you? Did you say *two hours*? Plus commute time? Plus time to get all dressed up? It's starting to sound like a part-time job."

9. **Word of Wisdom.** People will tell you they enjoy their harmless alcohol, vaping, or coffee. Or they might not believe they can overcome addictions to these substances, especially after years of use.

10. **Tithing.** People who are already struggling to make ends meet—or who wrestle with budgeting—don't see how they can make this kind of a financial commitment. Or, they don't see the need to turn their hard-earned funds over to what they view as a bureaucratic organization.

11. **Independence.** "It's my life and I'll live it the way I want." And, "My spouse (or kids) can do whatever. I'm fine the way I am." Some people just don't want to do what they don't want to do.

12. **Rejection of authority.** Some have an issue with anyone exerting authority over them. Rules may be "made to be broken." They don't want to be told they're accountable to someone.

13. **Affluence.** People who've worked hard to earn vacations, material things, and other worldly pleasures think they'll have to give them up.

14. **Acceptance.** "I don't think my friends would accept me if I joined your church. All I need is a reason for people to avoid me."

15. **No answers from God.** Some might expect a thunderous revelation or a specific sign, and they haven't experienced that—so they're convinced they haven't received an answer to a prayer about taking the next step.

16. **Temple commitments.** They may have misunderstandings about the temple, what goes on inside, and what kinds of commitments they'll have to make there.

17. **Church schedule.** They might say that church is too early in the day. Or they might say it's too late in the day and eats into their Sunday/family activities. Or maybe their work schedule conflicts with church attendance.

18. **The law of chastity.** People might not be ready to conform their lives to something so different than what the world allows.

19. **Hobbies**. The one thing they enjoy to unwind after a long week is their boxing class with their favorite instructor, who only teaches on Sunday mornings. They promised themselves they'd stick to this New Year's resolution.

20. **Organized religion**. Some believe religion is a deeply personal matter and doesn't need to be expressed to or in front of others. "My communion with God takes place on my hikes in the mountains."

Though not a scientific list, these are the very common concerns I've identified while working with many missionaries, less-actives, and investigators. For an exercise that's about to follow, you may choose to add others you come across, or to delete some of these if you think they don't apply in your situation.

Identifying concerns is essential as a preacher of the gospel. But be cautious. If you're not careful, you might find yourself being weighed down by all these concerns. They could adversely affect your view of what you're doing as a missionary. You might even begin to *believe* the negative concerns you're hearing.

Avoid interjecting negativity into your discussions, saying things like, "Yes, it's a big commitment to join the Church," or, "Yes, you do lose some friends when you obey the Word of Wisdom," or, "Yes, your family might reject you if you embrace the gospel." Comments like that may not be true. And besides, they are debilitating—to you and to your investigator.

Avoid getting too close to the "concern cliffs." You might find yourself even off-handedly remarking to your companion, "You know, he's right. We do expect people to change too quickly after they're baptized. Maybe we should just take it slower."

Or, "Despite her Word of Wisdom issues, I think if the mission president could relax the rules just a bit, she'd probably still make a great Relief Society teacher someday."

Or, "I think he makes a good point. What's wrong with taking your family to a movie on Sunday as long as you've gone to church first? After all, the family's spending time together, right?"

Never outwardly agree with an investigator's concern. As suggested earlier, as soon as you do, you validate that concern. You affirm in their mind that they really don't have to make commitments to the Lord or His servants. And that leads to shallow testimonies in uncommitted new members. Faith is a foundational requirement of any testimony. If they can't find and exercise faith in the commandments, it will be that much more difficult to do so with temple covenants.

Be watchful. Missionaries who begin to agree with investigators' concerns slowly begin to lose their standing as ministers of the Lord. They walk into the trap of carelessness and disregard for things holy and inspired. That might be one of the things Nephi was talking about when he warned us to not let Satan lead us "away carefully down to hell" (2 Nephi 28:21).

Find Positives for Every Negative

How do you protect yourself from being pulled down by these concerns—what we'll call *negatives*? Replace them with positives.

Isaac Newton's famous law of motion saw that for every action there is an equal and opposite reaction. When it comes to the concerns of investigators, that might as well be stated as, "Every negative has a positive." In other words, beneath every negative concern you hear, you should be able to glean something positive *about* the person who's saying it.

You might not always say a positive out loud. Sometimes you'll simply think or contemplate it in your mind. But whenever you sense it should be stated out loud, do it.

Let's look at how finding positives works.

Suppose the investigator's concern is with the law of chastity. He might say something like, "You're telling us that because we live together, we have to get married before we can be baptized? I mean, that's a huge commitment. I love her and all, but that's a big step to take."

His stated concern is that he's not ready to obey the law of chastity. That's the negative. Let's look at some positive things we might infer from his comment, however.

1.   He understands the importance of commitment.
2.   He doesn't take marriage lightly, which says a lot about his loyalty. At least he doesn't say, "Oh, sure, we'll get married" while thinking, *No problem. If it doesn't work out, I can just leave her.*
3.   He loves his girlfriend. If you listened empathically (to understand, not to respond), he said he loved her but didn't know if he was ready to get married. That's the opposite of saying, "Well, I don't think this is going to last very long. I'm not that attached to her."

Now let's suppose, following your clarifying, that the investigator elaborates on the concern and says, "I've got a brother who got married too early. He and his wife had three kids and then got divorced. In my opinion, they shouldn't have gotten married that soon; they didn't really know each other very well, and now things are a mess. I'm not going to commit to marriage if I can't be sure this thing is going to last and that I can provide for a stable family."

Whew. What kind of positives can you gather from that statement?

1.   He has values.
2.   He believes in strong and committed families.

3. He cares about the welfare of children.
4. He respects marriage as an important union.
5. He wants to be a provider.
6. It's unlikely he would ever want to hurt his wife, mentally or physically.

Think what would happen if, after he shared with you his concern (false or true, it really doesn't matter), you responded instantly with a positive statement about *him*. Pick any of those positives above and say something like, **"I really appreciate, Brother Giles, the respect you hold for marriage and the commitment you undoubtedly have for families."** Do you suppose this might encourage further dialogue between you and Brother Giles? Is he more likely to share more of his thoughts and feelings with you? Wouldn't he be more open, then, to receive your further counsel and advice as one of the Lord's servants? Because you found the positive in what many would view as a negative, you're agreeable without agreeing.

So, do you know where I would go next with this man? In other words, the *solutions* I'd begin to offer up for his concern? With some wise counsel from local Church leaders and perhaps a reliable fellow-shipper (preferably a happily married brother), this investigator is a serious prospect for marriage.

Present Solutions

Look at the title of this chapter again "Skill 4: Proper Listening to Resolve Concerns." This skill involves the ability to listen and solve—or resolve—concerns.

What's the difference between a positive and a solution? A positive is an *assumption* you're making about a person based on what he is telling you. (Positive assumptions are always advisable.) You can think of the positives silently, or you might articulate them to the investigator if you think it's appropriate and helpful for the relationship.

Solutions, then, are *ideas, suggestions,* or *additional information* you introduce. Recommendations, really. You're entitled to suggest solutions by virtue of being called to teach the gospel and represent the

Lord. Solutions involve the investigator, you, the Church, its members, and any other authorized resource you determine.

Sometimes your solution is nothing more than giving the investigator new information he didn't have. You live and breathe the gospel and the culture of the Church every day. Your investigator doesn't. Many concerns can be solved easily with a little more information or a better explanation of information you've already given. While certain things may be obvious to you, they're not to an investigator. After teaching the obvious, don't be surprised to hear, "Wow, I didn't know that. You mean it's really that simple?"

Maybe you and your companion can list all the tools, programs, people, scriptures, examples, and quotes you have that might help overcome any particular concern. You'll be amazed at how much the Lord has blessed us with to overcome our—and others'—challenges!

Bringing it All Together: Clarify, Find a Positive, Present a Solution

Just like the gospel itself, teaching the gospel should not be complicated. Though we've spent several pages on the topic of listening and resolving concerns, let's briefly summarize what we've learned and how to put it into action.

You know that people would rather be understood than be right. And as an ordained minister with the duty to help gather Israel, you can do your part by listening to the concerns or hesitations of Heavenly Father's children and helping them resolve those concerns so they can enter the covenant path.

This isn't done by beating them up and making them feel guilty. It's done by lovingly listening to understand (clarify), finding, and hopefully stating a positive from what they say; then providing a solution to get them where they need to be.

The journey to place them on the covenant path is filled with information—yours and theirs. While you will eventually share your information, for now it's your responsibility to find out all you can about *them*. And you'll get more information when you clarify, because people will want to elaborate when the listener is genuine and empathic. As they expound on their feelings, experiences, and circumstances, you'll get a better picture of where they're coming from—something that will more readily help you identify the positives and possible solutions.

You might discover that a funny thing happens as you clarify. The investigator may quickly realize, as you ask her to expand on her thoughts, that she's never really voiced the concern before—and now that she says it out loud, she might say something like, "Wait, that's kind of silly, isn't it? In the grand scheme of things, it really doesn't seem like that big of a deal. I mean, I'm letting a cup of hot black water laced with chemicals get in the way of my and my family's salvation? I really don't want to do that. When I say it out loud, I realize I can do better."

Look at the following example and see how the skill of listening and resolving concerns works.

Imagine you have an investigator who has said to you, in private, that he isn't enjoying his family. When he comes home each night, he feels that all the responsibilities are on his shoulders. He has to pick up all the pieces and solve all the problems. It's a constant burden. He's discouraged.

Though it may be hard to see at first, there are some obvious positives there. The investigator still loves his family—he's still providing for them, and they're still together. The kids will grow up appreciating their dad. When they have families of their own, perhaps they'll remember the importance of raising and caring for a family.

There are even some positives related to the shortcomings. The kids are seeing a father who fulfills his obligations—he goes to work every day, and he returns home every night. His example is teaching them a good work ethic and loyalty. He understands and honors his responsibility to provide for his family.

Instead of jumping right in and saying, "Let's talk about a program called family home evening," you might say something like, **"It's so impressive that you're such a diligent father and provider, that**

you go to work every day to meet your family's needs. You're obviously striving to create stability in your home."

State the positive in a sincere, gentle tone of voice, letting the investigator know immediately that you understand his concern. You're not agreeing that he has a dysfunctional family, but you're being agreeable.

This approach might feel awkward and uncharacteristic at first. But if you prayerfully ask the Lord to help you see the positive in every situation and every person you meet, you'll not only be a missionary with whom others want to associate, but you'll be one they can trust with their heartfelt concerns.

Once you've demonstrated trust by identifying and even stating the positives, continue by suggesting possible, inspired solutions.

One solution might be delegation—the principle of "return and report." He could give his children responsibilities—along with rewards—so they'll learn to work together and take some of the burden off him. Doing so would also help his kids learn self-reliance, not to mention how to contribute more to the family's needs. They would also be developing a good work ethic.

Yet another solution might be family prayer. By leading his kids in prayer, they can hear their dad express frustrations and hopes for each of them, opening up better communication and an avenue to talk about concerns.

Finally, consider Church programs or teachings that could serve as solutions. In this family's case, their daily conflict could be addressed by the family home evening program (and a fellowshipping family joining you and your companion to model one for them). But instead of immediately launching into an explanation of that inspired program in the first discussion, you first took the time to discover this investigator's needs and concerns so you would know the right positives and solutions to share. Now he finds those solutions relevant and applicable.

Solving with Stories

What happens when you've got a solution you're confident will help your investigator, but you're afraid of coming across as arrogant or pushy?

A helpful way is to share it through another's success story. Think of a success story as a *testimony*. You hear success stories regularly in testimony meeting. A person tells the congregation that she had a concern. An issue. A trial. And then she shares the solution: "I want to bear testimony that prayer helped me overcome my challenge." "I testify that reading The Book of Mormon gave me the answers I was looking for."

When you relay another person's success story, you not only help to humanize your investigator's own concern, but you set aside your personal opinion and bring others' ideas and successes into the picture. If there is "strength in numbers," allowing your investigator to see that others have shared the same concern helps them know that the gospel of Jesus Christ, His Atonement, and His Church addresses and solves all people's issues. A third-party success story aids your teaching.

This might sound strange, but think about taking notes in testimony meeting. Before long, you'll have a collection of real-life success stories that you can share—a variety of solutions and results others have obtained.

That can also happen when you invite members—all the way from recent converts to lifelong Latter-day Saints—to assist you in lessons. "Whenever possible invite members, preferably recent converts, to help you teach. . . . For example, have the members, as appropriate, share how they were able to learn, accept, and live a particular principle in the lesson. Have them explain how they made the decision to join the Church" (*Preach My Gospel*, 181).

President Thomas S. Monson also suggested inviting members to help you teach—something that not only benefits investigators but brings joy to the one helping you teach. You'll find an excerpt of the talk, which was delivered at a missionary training meeting, on page 181 of *Preach My Gospel*.

Another way to effectively deliver a solution is through a conversion story. You're a missionary, so you should know at least a few of those (including your own). It's easy to gather more. A companion study activity on pages 194–195 of *Preach My Gospel* suggests that you arrange to meet with a convert and ask about his or her conversion experience. Don't forget to ask lifelong members as well—remember that every member has a time when the Spirit revealed the truth. And those stories are powerful.

There are lots of uncomplicated ways to gather conversion stories. For example, whenever you have a dinner appointment with a member, make it a point to ask his or her conversion story. That can start as simply as asking, "What's your conversion story?"

Everyone loves stories. The Savior used them in His teaching. He knew that stories help people grasp a concept, relate to a principle, and apply it in their own lives. As a missionary, you should use everyday stories to teach the same way.

Think about your favorite general conference talks; chances are, they were filled with stories. Like all good stories, the ones you use to deliver solutions must have a beginning ("Here's the problem someone else faced"), a middle ("Here's how we worked together to overcome it"), and an end ("Here's the result she's now enjoying").

Deliver Stories with Empathy

As you compile and begin using success stories, deliver them with empathy. Meaning, remember that stories are highly personal. If someone bares their soul and tells you of a personal revelation, or how they were liberated through repentance, don't treat it casually.

Yes, sometimes you'll learn of a story and you'll need to keep the person's name confidential. Other times, it may be perfectly appropriate to share the name. Use your best judgment. You might even want to ask the subject of a story if it's okay to share their experience with others: "Would it be okay if I told people of your story? I know it could help to uplift and encourage others." If that person is willing, ask them to accompany you on the lesson—a member exchange. This could be the start of great fellowshipping.

As you convey another's story to an investigator, don't trivialize it by saying something like, "I know how you feel. Matter of fact, someone else I knew in my last area felt the same way, but he found it's really not that big of a deal." That's the opposite of empathy. It indicates the selfish attitude of someone who just wants to put a bandage on it and move on from someone's concern.

Delivering a story with empathy is extremely effective—as long as you're genuine. (If you attempt empathy for manipulation, your efforts will fail.) Sincerity, combined with the Spirit, will make this an effective tool for helping investigators overcome concerns. They will begin to learn the principle of "bear[ing] one another's burdens, that they may be light" (Mosiah 18:8).

Let's give a quick illustration. Suppose a concern comes from a woman who has a problem with Church leadership. You've already articulated positives to her; for example, she probably has a strong sense of right and wrong and feels confident in her ability to choose accordingly. Now you're ready to share some solutions.

Relate to the Investigator's Feelings

Say something like, "Sister Brown, I understand how you feel." The key words here are *understand*, something you can do only after thoroughly clarifying her concern, and *feel*, which suggests that what she's thinking is very real to her (even though it may not be a fact). You shouldn't *agree* by suggesting, "Oh, I totally know what you mean. A lot of our leaders appear like they just want to be in charge."

When you say, "I understand how you feel," you're demonstrating empathic listening.

Share a True Story

Having demonstrated empathic listening—which includes careful clarifying—share a true story by saying something like, **"I understand how you feel. In fact, someone else we were teaching a few**

months ago felt the same way." You're letting Sister Brown know that her concern isn't new or strange—you've taught another who shared similar feelings.

Be careful, though. Convey a level of understanding without suggesting that there is a widespread outbreak of this concern. You don't want to suggest that her concern is so prevalent that you're regularly inundated with it. Sometimes, in our desire to sound relatable, we carelessly come across as, "If I had a dime for everyone who has problems with 'the powers that be' in our Church, I'd be living in a mansion by now!"

Then share a true story by saying something like, **"Someone else we were teaching a few months ago felt the same way. And when he took some time with us to watch our leaders speak at our general conference last April, he found them to be amazingly loving, humble, and concerned for people all over the world–not just members of our Church. In fact, he found their messages inspiring, as though they were speaking directly to him. Our friend is already inviting his brother to his home later this year to watch the next general conference because he believes it will help his little brother get through some challenges he's going through, too."**

(Notice above that you should use the word *found* instead of *found out* ["What our other investigator found is that our leaders . . ."]. When you say someone *found out* something, it sounds too much like you were withholding information they had to "find out" later on their own. No one likes to feel information was withheld from them.)

Offer a Solution and a Result

Now bring the discussion back to her by testifying what will happen if she makes a similar choice as the person in the story you just told. Offer her a solution—one of many possible solutions—with a corresponding promised result.

Here's how that might sound: **"So, Sister Brown, I believe you'll find that your view of the leaders in our Church will be very similar to the friend I just told you about. You will see them as representatives of**

God in your life. I invite you to watch a few select talks they've given recently. We'd be pleased to show you online where you can find their teachings, and how they address issues that are especially relevant to you and your situation."

People need to be told the blessings they can receive if they put their trust in the Lord and take the same steps others have taken. Let them know that the Lord expects them to "Choose you this day" (Joshua 24:15). Encourage people to commit *today*—not tomorrow, not next week, not next month. After all, blessings await those who make commitments to the Lord, and you don't want to delay such a gift.

You might ask: if I don't have a legitimate success story to share, should I make one up?

No. A story will become a gimmick if it's not based on truth and empathy. Besides, you know how quickly the Spirit will leave if you resort to falsehoods or exaggerations simply to satisfy your own needs.

So, if you're new to the mission field, or just haven't accumulated any stories to share, try one of these suggestions:

- Use a success story from a companion or other missionary. Ask them, especially your trainer, **"Will you share with me your five best success stories from your mission so far?"** Or, **"What were the five toughest concerns you've helped others overcome?"** Their stories then become your stories and your teaching tools. Remember, these are first and foremost the Lord's investigators, not yours or theirs. It's perfectly appropriate to refer to another's experience by saying, **"We have an investigator,"** or **"We know of someone,"** or **"Our mission taught a family . . ."**

- If you know a personal story of a friend, relative, or acquaintance back home that's pertinent to the situation you're encountering, use it. No one says the story has to come from within your mission boundaries.

- Use your own story if it will help convey a principle to your investigator. You could say something like, **"You know what? I had this challenge [or misunderstanding] before I became a missionary, before I even joined the Church. Let me share with you how I resolved it and what it's done for me since."** However, be careful not to utilize repentance stories from your own life that may cast doubt or suspicion on the worthiness and appropriateness of the Lord's servants. When Alma the Younger taught, he didn't recount the details of all his nastiness, only that he understood sin because he had experienced it (see Mosiah 27:28–29). Our job is to uplift and focus on building trust, not to parade our every fault and weakness in front of earnest investigators.

In Chapter Seven we talked about inviting the investigator to make a commitment during and/or as your lesson concludes. In this chapter we've reviewed suggestions on how to listen and resolve any concerns that may come up as a result of your invitation to make that commitment.

After you've uncovered any true concerns and offered some solutions (perhaps with a success story of another person), the time has come to extend the ultimate invitation.

Chapter Nine

Skill 5: Opening the Gate to the Covenant Path

"As our faith in Jesus Christ grows, God invites us to make promises with Him. These covenants are manifestations of our conversion. . . . Covenants anchor us to the Savior and propel us along the path that leads to our heavenly home."

Elder Dale G. Renlund,
"Unwavering Commitment to Jesus Christ," *Ensign*, November 2019

Baptism is the first ordinance on the covenant path to Jesus Christ and His kingdom. Your ultimate goal as a missionary is to invite and assist His children onto that path.

Preach My Gospel suggests, "At the conclusion of each teaching visit, provide the people you teach with something to read and ponder in preparation for the next meeting. . . . The people you teach should always be given something to think about, to ponder, and to pray about. This can become an opening topic of discussion the next time you meet" (*Preach My Gospel*, 191).

In other words, at the end of every visit, give the investigator something to do. Don't just close your books and say, "Well, that was a nice discussion. Thank you for participating. When can we come back and do it again?"

That's not enough.

181

By giving investigators something to do and by asking for a commitment, you aid their continuation of spiritual momentum, and begin to train them to progress on their own. After all, you won't be there forever. Missionaries are transferred. Missionaries go home. But the Spirit and gospel study habits can stay with investigators if they do the things you counsel them to do. Even if they don't yet have the gift of the Holy Ghost, they have the power of the Holy Ghost to help and guide them.

Following Up on Commitments

It's important to see commitments through to completion. When you do, it shows that the Lord's representative is serious about and interested in an important pledge the investigator made. *Preach My Gospel* teaches, "Extending and following up on commitment invitations is vital because . . . [k]eeping commitments prepares people to make and keep sacred covenants" (*Preach My Gospel*, 198).

A commitment is nothing more than a preparatory covenant, isn't it? By helping people make and keep commitments, you are training them to establish a pattern of commitment making, or covenant making, in their lives. That will serve them well later as they prepare to enter the temple to receive additional ordinances that qualify them for exaltation. "We qualify for *that* privilege," taught President Russell M. Nelson, "by making covenants with God, keeping those covenants, and receiving essential ordinances" (Russell M. Nelson, "Come, Follow Me," *Ensign*, November 2018). Baptism is the first necessary ordinance.

What if someone, on the way to the path, makes a commitment to the Lord, through you, and when you meet again you find they have not kept the commitment?

Is that frustrating?

Of course! But there are specific things you can do to make that less likely.

Teaching Investigators to Keep Commitments

Imagine that you and your companion are meeting with Brother and Sister Gregson and their two children after dinner. As you wrap up the discussion, you invite them to make a certain commitment: "In preparation for our next visit, which we're hoping can be tomorrow night, please read 3 Nephi 11 along with the promise of the Book of Mormon. All right? Then we will talk about what you've read when we come back."

Let's look at that. **First, you asked for a very simple commitment**—read two sections of the Book of Mormon. You make sure your request is clear. In addition to marking where the scriptures are found, you might even give them prompts about what they should be considering as they're reading.

Second, confirm their intent to follow through. How? Perhaps you could say:

"Brother Gregson, Sister Gregson, we want you to be happy, and we believe that by reading these two parts, you'll receive a testimony of the things we've been discussing tonight–which will lead to true happiness. As you do, the Spirit will confirm to you that these things are true."

Then ask a direct question: **"Is there anything that could keep you from accomplishing this task before our next visit?"** If they say yes, they're sharing a concern with you. Or, you might ask: **"What obstacles–if any–might prevent you from accomplishing that before our next visit?"** If they bring up a roadblock, they're disclosing a concern. Either way, from what you've already learned, you know how to listen (clarify) and solve concerns.

Maybe it's a small concern: "You know, we are so busy at work, and our kids have activities at school tomorrow that we're attending, so I just don't think we'll be able to do it between now and tomorrow night." Or, "I have to get up early in the morning. I'm going to bed as soon as you leave tonight, so I won't be able to read."

A legitimate, simple concern like those doesn't necessitate a lot of solution—it just means adjusting your challenge. "Let's do it by the day after tomorrow, then, instead of by tomorrow. Does that work?"

They might still say no: "No, I don't think we can do that, because . . ." If you listen properly, you'll hear another concern. Maybe it's "We don't read very fast," or, "We're just not sure we should continue. You know, our pastor was quite upset when he learned we're meeting with you."

When you hear the true concern, try to solve it right then. There's no point in trying to get them to meet your commitment of reading 3 Nephi 11 if there's something preventing them from doing so. Figure out what the concern is and resolve it.

Now imagine Brother Gregson says, "No, I don't think there's anything that would keep us from doing that. I think we can do it. Yeah, we . . . we can make the effort."

Now go on to the next commitment: **set up your follow-up appointment**, which might be tomorrow night or two nights from now. Say something like, "May we come by tomorrow night at 7:30?"

Here we come to the crux of commitment-making: **the mutual commitment**. It's just what it sounds like—you include yourself in the commitment process.

If you give an investigator an assignment, he's more likely to fulfill it if he knows he's not the only one being asked to do something. He'll feel a lot more committed if he knows you're also going to be doing something between now and the next time you meet with him. The whole process reinforces trust and introduces accountability.

Here's how it would work with the Gregson family. First, review their assignment to read 3 Nephi 11 and Moroni 10:3–5. You could say something like:

"Thanks for allowing us to visit with you again tomorrow night. We'll be here at 7:30. If it's all right, we may bring along a member of our church–who, by the way, is an electrician, too. Since you've been in that line of work for years, Brother Gregson, we think Brother Davis would really enjoy meeting you.

So, between now and tomorrow night, please make sure you each read these two important scriptures. Then think about what you've read and how those passages apply to your situation today. We encourage you to pray, asking Heavenly Father to help you understand what He wants you to learn from them. In the meantime, my companion and I are going to . . ."

Here it comes—the second part of the mutual commitment:

". . . read those same verses. We're also going to ponder them and discuss them together. We'll be praying, too, to see if we can get even greater insights into those verses and how they apply to you and your family. And when we visit with you tomorrow night, we want to share with you some of the insights we're sure the Spirit will give all of us through this same exercise."

See what happened there? You've given yourselves an assignment—a task to fulfill. That makes it clear to your investigators you're not just going back to your apartment, kicking your feet up, enjoying some late-night ramen, and spending a relaxing day tomorrow while they're doing all the work reading, pondering, and praying about scriptures. Instead, you've shown your commitment to them—shown that your desire to help them is serious enough that you're going to make an effort, too.

And here's a bonus: you're asking Brother and Sister Gregson to report back to you next time they see you. Because you've made a mutual commitment, everyone will have something to report and share. There's accountability from all parties.

As a way of preparing for any teaching situation, you and your companion should ask, "What are examples of assignments we can give ourselves, at a moment's notice, to demonstrate to our valued investigators that we are indeed going the extra mile for them? What can we commit to do to show that we're focused on results in our service?"

Something as simple as that is a wise use of companion study time. Make a list of "missionary commitments" so when you feel prompted to extend a commitment request to your investigator, you're prepared to also assign *yourself* a task.

Remember: most investigators won't know the efforts you make for them. Don't assume they know how hard you work to prepare. Tell them, **"We're doing (fill in the blank) to show our commitment to you."**

In every commitment you make, be reasonable. Stay within the boundaries of mission rules. And draw on the Spirit to guide you in making a missionary commitment that will inspire your investigators as it represents the love you and the Savior have for them.

What are examples of commitments you might make? You're probably already doing some of them. Maybe you offer to do some special preparation for the next discussion:

"Sister Lo, to make sure we're prepared for tomorrow night, my companion and I are going to look further into the topics we discussed today. We'll see if there are other scriptures we can share, or any statements from today's prophets that will help all of us learn this principle more completely."

You might also offer to follow up on something the investigator said:

"Sister Lunds, you asked a very interesting question earlier in our discussion. As I've thought about it, I'd like to ask your permission to talk about it more when we meet on Saturday. We'll commit to study it further. There are some additional resources I'd like to consult. So, when we meet next, we'll plan to share more information on this subject with you. Thank you for asking that question, by the way; it'll be good for us to put some extra time into this topic."

This kind of commitment shows that you're really listening to what your investigator is asking and offering. You never want to come across like your lessons are pre-scripted and inflexible. Missionaries should never respond to a question by saying something like, "Well, that really doesn't apply to what we planned to discuss tonight, so let's not worry about that."

While you may not want to address a particular topic before the investigator is spiritually prepared to hear it, a mutual commitment gives you a chance to say, **"That's a very insightful question. With your permission, we'd like to address it specifically in one of our next visits. May we take some time to prepare to do so?"** That says you're going to do some extra preparation on their behalf. You should never imply that you're not already spiritually prepared to teach, but you *can* commit to do some extra study or to discuss a certain gospel principle at length later on.

Here's another example of a missionary commitment: praying for your investigator.

"Brother and Sister Ballard, we want you to know that as soon as we leave your home tonight, you're going to be in our prayers. We're going to be praying that as you read these verses together, you'll receive the confirmation you desire, and you'll understand what your Heavenly Father wants you to know."

Still another commitment you could make is to call on certain members of your ward or branch who might have experienced something similar to what your investigator is going through or feeling.

"Sister Ford, we appreciate what you've shared with us, and I can't help but think of another individual who could relate well to what you're going through. Her name is Sister Hall, and with your permission, we'd like to ask if she'd be willing to share some solutions she's found helpful. In fact, I'm sure Sister Hall would really enjoy the chance to speak with you, if you think that might be helpful."

Another commitment would be to help an investigator with any temporal needs. If employment issues are getting in the way of living the gospel, you might say:

"You know, Dana, we have an employment specialist in our local church named Brother Collins who's specifically responsible for helping members either find or improve their employment. Would it be all right if we spoke with him first thing tomorrow morning to discuss what recommendations he might have? Maybe we could even ask that he speak with you."

Another approach might be, **"We have a local church facility that specializes in career training and workshops. We'll find out when the**

next session will be taking place and text that information to you right away."

Try taking on the same kind of commitment your investigator has agreed to. For example, if he's agreed to abstain from smoking for a day, you can agree to abstain from eating sweets for twenty-four hours. What a great way to demonstrate your willingness to sacrifice along with them.

A final idea to add to what you've already committed is to suggest holding your next meeting at the home of a ward member and to commit to making that happen:

"We'd like to ask the Poulsen family if we can meet at their home for our next discussion. Brother Poulsen is what we call a 'ward missionary,' and he's been set apart to work with the full-time missionaries in hosting discussions like this. I'm sure he'd love to meet you. So, if that's okay, we'll call him as soon as we return home tonight and ask when they could have us over. Besides, the father's story is one I think you'll really relate to, especially how he interacts with members of his extended family who are of a different faith."

All these commitments demonstrate that you and your companion are going above and beyond your investigator's expectations. A loving missionary would never say, "Brother and Sister Hoopes, you read 3 Nephi, and we'll text you in a day or so to see how it's coming." No. Your commitment must reflect an extra effort, because that's what the Savior would do. And that's what the Savior expects all of us to do all the time. It's a higher and holier way of teaching.

The mutual commitment is a small technique you can use to help your investigators learn the principle of return and report. Through it, they will also learn that "when we obtain any blessing from God, it is by obedience to that law upon which it is predicated" (D&C 130:21).

One last important note: when you return and report on your assignment—the commitment you kept out of love—be sure to elaborate on what you've done in their behalf. It's not boasting, it's returning and reporting. But, ". . . this love cannot come with expectations of repayment. It cannot be the kind of service that expects recognition, adulation, or favor" (Dieter F. Uchtdorf, "Your Great Adventure," *Ensign*, November 2019).

Graciously, let them know you've been thinking about and studying and praying for them. You may be the only one who has exerted this much effort to help them in their spiritual journey. We're not trying to win points, we're trying to solidify trust.

Then, the Follow-Up Visit

What does a successful follow-up visit look like?

After you greet the investigator, you might say something like, **"Brother and Sister Mitton, there are three reasons we came by today."**

First, thank them for your previous visit. Three quick examples come to mind:

"For us, our visit with you last night was so rewarding. We felt the Spirit in your home. We appreciated your willingness to share your feelings, thoughts, and concerns." Or,

"We really appreciate the scriptures we were able to read together. They strengthened our own testimonies and deepened our knowledge of the gospel." Or,

"Thank you for making the sacrifice to meet with us last night. We appreciate your time and thank you for turning off the television. That really helped bring the Spirit into the discussion."

Second, remind them of the commitment they accepted:

"We're excited tonight to learn how your reading went the last twenty-four hours. We're interested in your feelings, thoughts, and impressions after studying 3 Nephi 11 and the Book of Mormon challenge."

Third—and before they give you a report on their commitment—*report on what* you've *done since you last met* (which involves the commitment you made):

"And before we get an update on your reading of the Book of Mormon last night, we want to share with you what we've done since our last meeting." Or,

"Let me share with you the scriptures my companion and I studied this morning to prepare for tonight's discussion and the impression they left on us." Or,

"Let us share with you the conversation we had with our Primary president. We got some great insights from her on some activities your children might want to attend."

Remember, by sharing you're not trying to impress or get glory. The purpose is to articulate your feelings for them, your regard for them, your commitment to them. You want to be clear that you, as representatives of Christ, hold them in such high regard and value their studying the gospel so much that you've expended some extra effort.

After you give them an update on your assignment, turn your focus back on them. **"Now, back to the main purpose of our visit tonight: How was your reading of the Book of Mormon?"** Or,

"How is it going with your challenge with tobacco?" Or,

"How was your conversation with your spouse?" Or,

"What kind of feedback did you get from your roommates after we left last night?"

Regardless of what the assignment was, you're asking for a report—the principle of return and report. Notice that you should ask for their report only after you've given yours. Once you've done so, investigators will feel more responsible to share their report with you. If they didn't keep their commitment, they will feel more accountable to follow through the next time you assign them a reasonable task.

So, if in fact they *didn't* keep the commitment, what then? Don't beat them up over it. Don't look devastated. You don't stop the lesson and say, "Well, we're not going to continue tonight until you read 3 Nephi 11. We'll come back when you've done it. Should we give you a half an hour?" Yikes, no.

You recommit them. You re-challenge them. Remind them that the commitment is important, because it's not a commitment to you— it's a commitment to the Lord who loves them.

Commitments are important because they place people on the road to repentance. When someone falls through, then, you can be disappointed—not because he didn't do what you asked, but because he's not doing what's necessary to receive the great blessings that come with repentance. When you genuinely love someone, you'll naturally feel disappointed by their non-performance of vital steps towards happiness.

As you continue the lesson, you might be prompted by the Spirit to add another commitment to the list. But whether you give a second assignment or reiterate the first, make sure you give yourself and your companion another assignment, too. This won't be hard because you've already prepared several assignments you can always give yourselves at any time during or at the end of a discussion.

"No" Is Not Forever

As a missionary, you might be tempted to get discouraged when someone says, "No, I really don't think this is the right time for our family." Or, "Thanks for giving us this Book of Mormon. We'll keep it on our shelf, but we're not interested right now." Or, "We appreciate the invitation to come to church, but you know, we're busy for the next four Sundays with our boys' football games. Why don't you stop by in a month or so, and we'll revisit it then."

That "no" wasn't a forever answer.

Never forget: change happens. It's an eternal principle—things always change. The person who says "no" to you today could very well say "yes" to missionaries tomorrow, because something may happen to change her life. Her job may change. Her schedule could change. Relationships change. Her heart will change. Things happen. And that's what's beautiful about the nature of life and the continual movement of the gathering of the Lord's elect.

Who in scripture vehemently rejected the gospel but later accepted it? Alma the Younger. Zeezrom. Saul. The sons of Mosiah. The scriptures are full of examples of people who basically told the missionaries, "Get lost! Take your preaching elsewhere. I don't need it."

But because life brings change—no, because the Atonement of Jesus Christ is the basis for change—each of those people turned around to accept the gospel. In fact, some of them so enthusiastically embraced the gospel that they became among the greatest missionaries of all time.

Let me be clear: **"no" is not forever. "No" is for now.** If you accept that truth and never forget, you won't be bothered by rejection. You won't be afraid of it. You'll only feel sorrow for those who say it.

What do you do, then, when people say "no"? Say a silent prayer that their conditions in life will change and the "no" turns into a "yes." Then thank them for their time and leave something behind that they can always put on their fridge or on their desk to remember the experiences they had with the missionaries. Leave a Pass-Along card, a Book of Mormon, a brochure, or a tract—certainly a prayer. Provide some service—ask if there's anything you can do to serve them before you leave. How would Jesus depart?

When someone says "yes," you're harvesting, probably where someone else has planted. If someone says "no," you're planting seeds that another missionary might come across and water in the future. Either way, planting or harvesting, you're directing people to the waters of baptism. You are going about the Lord's business and inviting others to follow Him.

The Teaching Triangle

Let's go back to the name of this skill: "Opening the gate to the covenant path."

Whenever you open your mouth to teach, you're taking part in a teaching triangle. You're one side of that triangle; your investigator is another. But the Savior represents the critical third side of the triangle—and if He wasn't there, the triangle would collapse. Never forget that it's a triangle relationship, not a vertical one between you and the investigator. They're more likely to follow Christ as they see and hear you make and keep commitments to them, Him, and others.

Making commitments to investigators might have become such second nature that you might forget why you're doing it. But never forget: *They are an example of how the Savior makes and keeps commitments,* and another reminder that He is a constant, integral part of the teaching triangle.

You represent the Savior and are expected to love your investigators. But there's one area in which you *can't* substitute for the Savior—and that's in the development of your investigator's relationship with and devotion to Him. Always help investigators remember that Christ is the One who atoned for their sins. He is the One who makes covenants with His people. "Rarely, if ever, should you talk to people or teach them without extending an invitation to do something that will strengthen their faith in Christ" (*Preach My Gospel*, 198). He is the One with whom they should be building trust and allegiance.

Elder Dale G. Renlund taught, "Being 'converted unto the Lord' means leaving one course of action, directed by an old belief system, and adopting a new one based on faith in Heavenly Father's plan and in Jesus Christ and His Atonement" ("Unwavering Commitment to Jesus Christ," *Ensign*, November 2019).

As you invite and direct them towards the covenant path, you will witness the fruits of your labor. And since the "straight and narrow" path widens as more people walk it, you will want to encourage this new convert of Christ to bring others along.

Chapter Ten

Skill 6: Connecting through Referrals

"My heart reaches out to you missionaries. You simply cannot do it alone and do it well. You must have the help of others. . . . But you must do all you can."

President Gordon B. Hinckley,
"Find the Lambs, Feed the Sheep," *Ensign*, May 1999

What does President Hinckley mean by *all you can*? Part of it is doing all you can to become a more effective, Spirit-led teacher as we've discussed throughout these pages. And part of it is faithfully asking members for referrals and training them on how to give referrals comfortably.

What? you say. *Look, I love the members, but when it comes to getting referrals from them, I'd have more luck asking them to clean my apartment.*

Fair enough. So, where do we start?

First, to be comfortable giving a referral, members must be converted themselves. That is a subject for another time and place. But even for those who do have a firm testimony of the gospel of Jesus Christ and a love for their fellowmen, there are so many perceived hurdles to giving referrals that appear to be insurmountable. Will people misjudge their motivation? Will they harm a relationship? Will it lead to contention? Will they be able to answer tough questions? Will they be viewed as judgmental or holier-than-thou?

As ordained missionaries, you are specially qualified to help members realize these fears come from the adversary, who seeks "the misery of all mankind" (2 Nephi 2:18). As "a child of Christ," though, you and converted members "lay hold" on everything that's good (see Moroni 7:19). And when you find it, you are inspired to share it with others, regardless of worldly fears.

Of course, most members want to see their friends and family live with the joy they experience from the gospel. But they need help to take that step. Or, perhaps, they need some skills that will take them there. Here's how you can help.

Start by teaching them success stories that led to inspiring outcomes.

An investigator success story is an example of someone who's been through the missionary discussions, has accepted the gospel, has received baptism, and is now actively participating in the Church. Perhaps she has entered the temple and is advancing on the covenant path. If it's a brother, he might also be on the way to receiving the Melchizedek Priesthood. You can find these kind of success stories all around the Church.

Another type of success story is a member who gave you a referral that turned into a life-changing conversion. Share those experiences with every member. They will be more inspired to submit a referral on the Church website or give you a referral if they know the process transforms lives.

They think, "Wow, if she can do it, I can do it." "If he could talk about the gospel with his boss, I can do it with my colleague." "If she could introduce the Church to her agnostic neighbor, I can talk to my devout Presbyterian neighbor."

Along with sharing the success stories that lead to baptism, you might share another kind of success story—one that didn't produce a missionary lesson, but which expanded a friendship. I'm not kidding. Years ago, a ward mission leader wanted me to share with our ward members just that: "Hey, I tried, and it didn't work—this time. No's not forever. I understand that even though he didn't want to hear the discussions right now, things might change, and he might want to hear them sometime down the road. But you know what? It didn't hurt. I'm still alive. And my neighbor and I still visit in the street."

That's a success story because as a member, I still have that friendship. Members need to know that a referral that declines our offer does not have to lead to a damaged relationship.

A Rule for Obtaining Referrals

There's an important and counter-intuitive rule for missionaries about obtaining referrals from members: **give to get**.

What kinds of things should you give members? Give your time. Give attention. Give your testimony. All those things help build trust with members. When you give your best, members will talk among themselves. "Elder Haslem found out about that math test I aced." "Sister Wilkinson congratulated me on the award I got at work." "Elder Hoffman found out that I made the marching band." When you focus your time and attention on members, they will more likely focus their friends on you.

Full-time missionaries can also give service. You might ask, **"Is there anything we can do to support any of you in your callings?"** Or, **"Does anyone need any assistance in teaching a lesson?"** Or, **"Does anyone need help ministering to someone right now?"**

Don't do anything contrary to what your mission president directs, and always stay within the boundaries of the mission rules. But if you look for ways to serve, you'll find lots of opportunities within those rules. And when you help the members do their jobs, they'll want to help you do yours.

It's Christmastime all year: the more you give, the more you get back.

How to Ask for Referrals

This one's easy: **ask simple questions**.

Some questions sound deceptively simple but are actually complicated. Here's one: "So, Brother Jeppson, do you know anyone who might be interested in taking the missionary discussions?"

How does the member respond to that? "I don't know. I've never talked about missionary discussions with my friends."

Here's another example: "Brother Carl, do you know of anyone who is looking for a new church right now?"

How is a member likely to respond? "I have no idea!"

So how *do* you ask?

Just as you do when you teach, keep it simple. *Ask who in their circle of friends shares their interests.* For example, if you find out that a high priest in the ward plays on the city softball team, you might ask, **"Who are some of your best buddies on the softball team?"**

He won't have to think about that for a week (or more) and "I'll let you know." He can tell you immediately that Craig and Tim are his best friends on the softball team.

Or you might notice that a woman in the ward loves to do quilting. You could say, **"Sister Archibald, I notice you're into quilting. Do you quilt with other people in the neighborhood?"**

She can tell you right away, "Oh, yeah. I do it with Sue, a few doors down, and Nancy, who's right across the street. We get together every month and we have an all-day quilting party."

Here are some other examples:

"Are there other families in your neighborhood with kids in Little League?"

"When Allie was in the hospital for the birth of your child, did you get to know other dads?"

You see where this is going? Nobody has to think about it and maybe get back to you. You help them remember the names of people who are just like them, who may share similar interests or aspirations.

Here comes your follow-up question—the key to it all.

Don't ask, "Do you think they might be interested in hearing the missionary discussions?" Instead, you ask, **"Do you think Jason and Melanie would appreciate knowing how to make their family a forever family?"**

How do you think they're likely to answer?

Notice in that example you used the word *appreciate*, not *interested*. "Appreciate" is warm and encouraging. "Interested" asks someone to make a decision for somebody else.

Consider other examples:

"Do you think your friend with the marital problems would appreciate knowing how the Atonement of Jesus Christ can actually bring peace into her home right now?"

"Do you think your cousin would appreciate knowing why the passing of a loved one is only the next stage and not the end of family relationships?"

Put in such a way, what can a member say?

When you use the word *appreciate*, a member hears the question differently. Do you think it's likely that a member would respond with, "No, I don't think they'd appreciate knowing about what Christ's Atonement can do"? Or, "No, I really don't think they'd appreciate knowing that one day they can see their spouse again"?

Chances are, they will respond with something like, "Sure, I guess so. I mean, why not? You're not asking me if they'll be baptized, are you?"

"No," you gently say, **"I'm only asking if you think they'd appreciate knowing the same truths that give you peace and perspective."**

Show that You Value Their Referral

Obtaining more referrals requires that you show members how much you value their friends and loved ones.

One simple and effective way of doing that is to show urgency and care in contacting the referral: **"If you'd provide us their name and contact information, I promise we'll reach out to them right away."**

Please notice the word *promise* in that sentence. That's not done by accident, nor done lightly. The word *promise*—if you can keep it—is a sign of your seriousness and trustworthiness. Why not use a word that underscores your commitment? It will give the member greater confidence in you and your readiness to treat their friend or loved one honorably.

By the way, if a member wishes first to strategize with you or contact the friend together, that's great. Adjust, but don't delay.

Another way of showing appreciation is to take some time to get to know a little about the referral from the member. You might ask,

"How do you know Richard? Share a little with me about his background, and why do you think the gospel would be helpful to him right now?" You can also inquire about the referral's family, religiosity, occupation, interests . . . and any other relevant topic you think would help your preparation.

The more you know about the referral, the more likely you will approach that individual in an appropriate way and with an applicable benefit statement. The member will know that you value the trust they are placing in you. The less you know about the referral, the more likely you'll miss the mark. If the member thinks you're haphazardly going for a referral, he probably won't give you more referrals, let alone this first one.

But getting the name and introduction is only the beginning. *Make sure to follow up afterward with the member who gave you the referral.* After you've thoroughly assessed her friend, neighbor, family member, schoolmate, or colleague, make sure you keep her up to date on what's happening. The follow-up can be as simple as calling the member and saying something like, **"We stopped by Callie's house and had a good visit with her. We let her know of our interest in being her friend, and we bore simple testimonies on the benefits of faith."**

Even if things don't go well with a referral, still follow up with the one who gave it to you. They want and deserve to know. **"We wanted to keep you posted that we stopped by the Folkman home, but it looked like a bad time for them. We excused ourselves and told them we'd come back another time. We wanted you to be in the loop."** Share what was said, what wasn't said, what you gave them, and what you didn't have time to give them.

Members deserve the benefit of the doubt. They could be like the newly converted Lamanites in the fifteenth chapter of Helaman who, after receiving the Nephites' preaching, were "in the path of their duty . . . striving with unwearied diligence that they may bring the remainder of their brethren to the knowledge of the truth" (Helaman 15:5–6). They want to introduce you to those friends who are "in preparation to hear the word of God" (Alma 32:6), but you have to consistently demonstrate your readiness to receive.

You can show you're prepared by what happens every week in church. Members will watch how you interact, how you speak, how you carry yourself, the authenticity in your face, the energy in your body, your friendliness, the strength of your testimony—even where you sit. Are you aloof, or are you engaged? Do you shake hands and smile, or do you whisper with your companion as people are filing in?

If they like what they see, they will become convinced that you are a true representative of the Lord—someone who works through the Spirit. Someone who will not disappoint them. And they'll be willing, if asked properly, to give you a valuable referral.

Unfortunately, you might be serving in an area where previous missionaries messed around, didn't work very hard, spent a lot of time hanging around the basketball court or gaming center, or rarely interacted with the members. Or maybe when a member asked a missionary to read a scripture and share its meaning, the missionary seemed extremely unprepared—like he wasn't familiar with the scriptures. In that situation, your problem isn't the members; sadly, it's the missionaries before you.

Things like that—things that happened before you ever got there—can prevent members from giving you referrals. You'll have to work extra hard to overcome that stereotype and reestablish trust among the members. Pray for understanding, patience, and insight as to how you can rebuild trust in the area. Repair work sometimes takes longer than original construction, so vow that you will always be the missionary who leaves an area better than you found it—with stronger, more trusting relationships with the members and investigators.

I remember a missionary who was assigned to a ward where we lived. He demonstrated to me by the way he conducted himself that when I put him in front of my friends, I wouldn't regret doing so. I knew he was going to teach the gospel the way it should be taught—with energy, enthusiasm, and zeal. And he was worthy to have the Spirit accompany him.

I want to feel that way about every missionary who walks through the door of the chapel. I want *you* to be that in your current ward! I want *you* to be the one I'm finally going to be able to introduce to my neighbor. And I'm not alone. When you stand and introduce yourself for the first time, dozens—even hundreds—of members are silently asking themselves, *Is this the missionary I've been waiting for?*

When your mission president interviews you for the first time, he's also hoping you're the one. He's hoping you're the one who is going to raise the bar of performance for the entire mission. Don't let him down. Because when all is said and done, that's how you show the Lord you won't let *Him* down.

Chapter Eleven

Skill 7: Fellowshipping Effectively

"Now he that planteth and he that watereth are one: and every man shall receive his own reward according to his own labour. For we are labourers together with God."

Apostle Paul, 1 Corinthians 3:8–9

We're down to the last skill, and I'm guessing it's one you don't think about as much. Because it's not your role as a missionary to actively engage in fellowshipping.

Does that mean you're off the hook?

Absolutely not. Part of your missionary service is to teach ward members and leaders how to fellowship. After all, fellowshipping is just continuous teaching.

The Father said, "he that endureth to the end, the same shall be saved" (2 Nephi 31:15). Good fellowshipping can help a new convert—all of us, really—endure to the end. The Book of Mormon describes it as a part of the gathering: newly baptized brothers and sisters "being carried in [the members'] arms and upon [the members'] shoulders" on the covenant path (see 1 Nephi 22:8).

Fellowshipping, therefore, is critically important, and I hope to give you a little extra perspective of what you can be doing as a missionary to help ensure the success of your new converts as you hand them over to the ward. I'm going to base that perspective on a landmark talk by President Gordon B. Hinckley in which he explained that each new member of the Church needs three things (see "Find the Lambs, Feed the Sheep," *Ensign*, May 1999, 108; *Preach My Gospel*, 216).

Once you learn your role in those three responsibilities, you'll understand how you contribute to the sacred role of helping new members succeed and stay on the covenant path toward exaltation.

Every New Convert Needs a Friend

The first thing President Hinckley said every new convert needs is a friend in the Church. That should be a friend, President Hinckley said, "to whom he can constantly turn, who will walk beside him, who will answer his questions, who will understand his problems" ("Find the Lambs, Feed the Sheep," *Ensign*, May 1999, 108).

As a missionary, you can get the ball rolling. As you're teaching each investigator, be looking for the friend President Hinckley talked about. Watch for members of the ward who are likely to match our new convert in interests, in needs, in background, in occupation, or in family structure.

You should get to know the members in the ward so well that when you first meet an investigator, you immediately think of members who ought to get involved. Make them a part of the process as soon as you can. Their potential friendship will be stronger if they get in the boat *during* the investigator's conversion journey instead of meeting them when they land on shore.

Every New Convert Needs an Assignment

The second imperative for every new convert is an assignment. President Hinckley taught, "Activity is the genius of this Church. It is the process by which we grow. Faith and love for the Lord are like the muscle of my arm. If I use them, they grow stronger. If I put them in a sling, they become weaker. Every convert deserves a responsibility" ("Find the Lambs, Feed the Sheep," 108).

So how on earth do you as a missionary make that happen?

Here's an example. A missionary who had been in our ward only three weeks found me in the hallway and asked how a recent convert was doing. In the course of our brief conversation, I mentioned that the convert didn't yet have a calling. The missionary said, "You know where he'd be great?" and he gave me a suggestion. As a member of the ward council, I was able to take a thoughtful suggestion and help make it a reality.

Your job as a missionary is not to receive revelation for callings in the ward. But it's completely appropriate for you to make well-considered recommendations, especially involving new converts. You may know that person better than anyone, since you've been teaching him. What kind of calling might you suggest for that convert?

Just remember—and you already know this: the bishop has the authority, the stewardship, and the mantle to receive the revelation for callings. He's always looking for information, though, that may precede that revelation. And that's exactly what you can provide.

But it's just a recommendation—one of many, perhaps, he's getting from members of his council. As he prayerfully seeks guidance, the bishop may or may not act on your suggestion. Never be offended if he doesn't. Like the Lord does and will do with you, the bishop is entitled to see the bigger picture for his flock.

Every New Convert Needs to Be Nourished by the Word

Third, and last, President Hinckley pleaded, "Every convert must be 'nourished by the good word of God' (Moro. 6:4). It is imperative that he or she become affiliated with a priesthood quorum or the Relief Society. . . . He or she must be encouraged to come to sacrament meeting to partake of the sacrament, to renew the covenants made at the time of baptism" ("Find the Lambs, Feed the Sheep," 108).

As you entrust your new convert to the ward, keep your eyes and ears open "to keep them in the right way, to keep them continually watchful unto prayer, relying alone upon the merits of Christ" (Moroni 6:4). Make sure the members are following through by inviting her to gospel discussions, meetings, sitting by her, and helping her feel a part of what's going on. If that's not happening, do what you can to encourage the leaders of your ward and other members to help.

Conclusion

Simply put, fellowshipping is ministering to new members. As a full-time missionary, you learn ministering skills that will serve you well throughout your life. And as Elder Dieter F. Uchtdorf taught, "There is something interesting, almost paradoxical, about this path you've chosen: the only way for you to progress in your gospel adventure is to help others progress as well" ("Your Great Adventure," *Ensign*, November 2019).

Those "others" are not just your dear investigators, they are the member missionaries of the Church who need the benefit of your spirit, your patience, and your vision of the work as you play an important role in *their* gospel adventure.

Chapter Twelve

Concluding Thoughts:
"Thou Shalt Speak"

"Therefore, my beloved brethren, be ye steadfast, unmoveable, always abounding in the work of the Lord, forasmuch as ye know that your labour is not in vain in the Lord."

Apostle Paul, 1 Corinthians 15:58

There's no question about it. Missionary work is hard.

If it wasn't, more religions would be doing it.

But missionary work can be made easier if you work individually and as companions to practice and master the fundamental skills of your calling. By knowing the principles of the gospel and vigilantly remaining united with the Holy Ghost, you can adopt and apply better teaching skills to your labors.

Missionary work is made easier by understanding that things your investigators are searching for are found in the gospel message you carry. You're not asking investigators to abandon their personal objectives—instead, you're teaching them how to use the gospel to achieve those outcomes better than before. As investigators are baptized, they should recognize and look forward to the wonderful results awaiting them.

Do you realize that when you bear testimony, you're testifying of the results you're obtaining from living the gospel? The gospel is the best way to receive long-lasting results. This is vital for investigators to realize. Their testimonies must be grounded in the principles of the gospel that produce sustainable results, not dependent on the changing programs of the Church.

Because before long, as all new converts discover, trials will arise. Some are large, some are small. Some concern their personal life; some relate to their membership in the Church or to the Church as a whole. There may be personality conflicts or small differences in administrative methods. And there may be challenges related to callings—getting them or being released from them.

When any such unexpected or unwelcome changes happen in the life of converts who are grounded in the gospel, their testimonies won't go up and down with the announcements or mechanics of the Church. Instead, they'll be rooted in the more important results they're getting from living the gospel.

Upon arriving in the Americas following His Resurrection, the Savior instituted a higher law, though the people had been taught and were accustomed to their customs of the law of Moses. He was making them holier when He said, "Therefore those things which were of old time, which were under the law, in me are all fulfilled. Old things are done away, and all things have become new" (3 Nephi 12:46–47).

Similarly, in our day, President Russell M. Nelson has led the Church into a "higher and holier way" ("Opening Remarks," *Ensign*, November 2018). Practices may change, but the principles of the gospel are constant. "Continually holding fast" (1 Nephi 8:30) to that rod, despite the scoffing and mocking of an unstable world, will lead us to God.

Immerse investigators in this principle. As you do, you'll see more effective and productive members of the Church. Retention and commitment to their new covenants will intensify. Remember, too, that inviting someone to accept baptism is not the end of anything. When they take that first step on the covenant path, it's the *beginning* of everything they hold dear.

The Savior said:

Come unto me, and be baptized in my name, that ye may receive a remission of your sins, and be filled with the Holy Ghost, that ye may be numbered with my people who are of the house of Israel (3 Nephi 30:2).

From the time I jotted down the first word of this book, my sincere goal has been to 1) make a small contribution to further arm the Lord's ambassadors so that 2) more doors can be opened, and 3) the gospel can penetrate more hearts, and 4) more lives can be improved. I have placed before you a set of principles, truths, and skills that I humbly pray can assist in making you an even better servant of the Lord.

But these same skills, which I am grateful God has introduced to me through so many means, will go far beyond your eighteen- or twenty-four-month mission. Diligent application of these skills will make you a more dignified priesthood holder, a more converted servant, a more understanding husband or wife, a more patient mother or father, a more caring leader, a more exemplary professional, and a more faithful Latter-day Saint. These skills will bless your life for life.

As a young missionary in the Missionary Training Center, I had an experience that buoyed me up when I needed it most. As you now know, my assignment was to serve the Japanese people. And while I was eventually able to communicate in their language with some confidence, it took time, prayer, and great effort to obtain that blessing. One night, while sitting on the hallway floor of the MTC dormitory, I randomly opened my scriptures to find a familiar seminary mastery scripture, and read:

Then the word of the Lord came unto me, saying,
Before I formed thee in the belly I knew thee; and before thou camest forth out of the womb I sanctified thee, and I ordained thee a prophet unto the nations. (Jeremiah 1:4–5)

I knew those verses well. I had learned that this passage proved foreordination and the existence of life before birth.

But that night in the MTC dorm hallway, I kept reading. As I did, I found Jeremiah articulating the very struggle I was caught up in:

> Then said I, Ah, Lord God! behold, I cannot speak: for I am a child.
>
> But the Lord said unto me, Say not, I am a child: for thou shalt go to all that I shall send thee, and whatsoever I command thee *thou shalt speak.*
>
> Be not afraid of their faces: for I am with thee to deliver thee, saith the Lord. . . .
>
> And the Lord said unto me, Behold, I have put my words in thy mouth. (Jeremiah 1:6–9; emphasis added)

Despite any weaknesses you might have, you are commanded, as was Jeremiah, to speak. You will or have been set apart to preach the eternal gospel of Jesus Christ. Preaching requires building trust, assessing personalities and needs, tailoring your message, listening and resolving honest concerns, and then, as instructed by the Spirit, speaking and teaching with skill and boldness.

***

You are a "fellow missionary" with the Lord's apostles. You have access to instruction and guidance in the scriptures and through the teachings of prophets. You have the support of others who testify alongside you. You have the companionship of the Holy Ghost and are assisted by angels. You're the subject and beneficiary of countless prayers in closets and in holy places. You are sustained by strong, capable leaders locally and worldwide, as well as an entire Church that was restored to prepare the world for the Second Coming of Jesus Christ.

You're standing on the shoulders of your predecessors—hundreds of thousands from whose successes and disappointments you can learn. You possess skills and resources that separate your training and methods from the world and its ways.

Hands of authority, laid upon your head and possessing the power of the priesthood, give you heaven-sent promises that are very personal to you. All you need to do to claim those promises is commit energy and dedication and use teaching skills to "match your message."

I admire you for accepting this noble call. I testify that you are assisting in Jesus Christ's most important latter-day work. I testify, too, that the Father will refine your teaching and consecrate your efforts in His own time so long as your intentions are pure and your faith is steady. And I pray that as you prepare and live as one of His elect disciples, His sweetest blessings will always be upon you and the people you are sent forth to love and serve.

Appendix A

Preparing Tomorrow's Missionaries Today

Teaching Skills for Disciples of Christ

A Summary

Preface

Missionaries of the Church of Jesus Christ of Latter-day Saints are disciples of Christ who teach His truth. Using the guidance and wisdom found in *Preach My Gospel* and from Church leaders, "Preparing Tomorrow's Missionaries Today" brings practical ideas to pre-mission teens and other interested parties who want to develop skills commensurate with this sacred charge.

SECTION I: Principles and Practices

Chapter One: "Proclaim His Gospel"— Teaching to Match Our Message

To proclaim suggests that one must speak. Therefore, regardless of their assigned area of service, missionaries are commissioned with learning the "language of the Lord" and articulating it so the world can understand. To be successful, they must recognize the power of persuasion, influence, and convincing—effective missionary traits throughout time. We discuss how these can be applied without manipulation or self-serving tactics.

This chapter also addresses: 1) the necessity of the Holy Ghost's companionship; 2) the requirement of gospel knowledge; and 3) the ability to confidently communicate what the Spirit and gospel require.

Chapter Two: What to Know Before Saying a Word

Despite the world's many enticements, all of God's children fundamentally want the same things. Miraculously, these objectives are obtainable through the gospel of Jesus Christ. We dive into this principle and clearly show how missionaries can help all of God's children achieve what they believe to be most important. Rather than preach or convert investigators to His Church, we emphasize the results (blessings) available through membership in His Church.

Chapter Three: Principles for Proclaiming

Missionaries focus on four principles to make their teaching more powerful and effective: 1) focus on results for the investigator; 2) do what successful missionaries do or have done; 3) do not distract from the Spirit; and 4) proclaim with urgency.

Chapter Four: Your Voice Is Your Suit

A disciple's message is the good news of Christ. The way it's delivered reflects its value and the sacred responsibility of the messenger. Missionaries, therefore, must be bold without being overbearing. They recognize that when they speak the words of the Spirit, they are vocalizing God's message to the investigator. This chapter is dedicated to providing practical tools to "open our mouths" with care, conviction, and courage.

SECTION II: Seven Skills of a Successful Missionary

While never replacing the counsel of Church leaders, mission leaders, *Preach My Gospel*, and the scriptures, missionaries should develop a mastery of seven essential skills to aid their work.

Chapter Five: Skill 1—Knowing How to Build Trust

In this age of cynicism, doubt, and despair, disciples of Jesus Christ must be trusted to be believed. Intuitive and effective techniques are illustrated to give missionaries the tools necessary to more quickly open hearts, minds, and doors. We explore various approaches—including key words that help our attempts—that resonate with investigators and members alike to establish trust with missionaries.

Chapter Six: Skill 2—Assessing for Understanding

Missionaries learn that though the gospel is the same, investigators are not. Each has their own interests, achievements, needs, and concerns. Learning what they are can be difficult, time-consuming, and intimidating to young disciples. How to ask appropriate, thoughtful, and relevant questions is the aim of this chapter. Readers will learn what information propels conversation towards conversion.

Chapter Seven: Skill 3—Presenting a Tailored Message

As they follow the Spirit, missionaries are able to prepare messages suited to their investigator. We explore techniques to help teachers customize lessons that will convince the listener that God knows them and their individual needs or desires. Staying true to the prescribed concepts in missionary lessons, insights as to how they are best adopted and received is the focus of this chapter.

Chapter Eight: Skill 4—Proper Listening to Resolve Concerns

Ordained ministers of Jesus Christ emulate not only His teaching, but His desire and ability to understand individuals' doubts. Recognizing that stated concerns often cover fears, the trained missionary will see each question as an invitation to respectfully clarify so they can offer loving solutions. This chapter is centered on how missionaries can address today's most common concerns associated with entering the covenant path.

Chapter Nine: Skill 5—Opening the Gate to the Covenant Path

As investigators learn to keep commitments, they practice the eternal pattern of covenant-making. The missionary will learn in this chapter how to extend meaningful commitments while modeling the principle of "return and report." Techniques in patient persistence are taught so as to help investigators feel God's love while understanding that accountability is a part of personal discipleship.

Chapter Ten: Skill 6—Connecting Through Referrals

In order to obtain something of value—such as member referrals—missionaries must first give something of value to members. How and what to give to earn members' trust is an essential part of this skill. Then, asking in such a way that names and faces come instantly to the member missionary's mind is a technique that serves both the giver and the receiver.

Chapter Eleven: Skill 7—Fellowshipping Effectively

Newly baptized members are unlikely to enjoy all the blessings of the gospel of Jesus Christ unless they are welcomed by current members who are themselves enduring to the end. Missionaries, skilled in how to engage with truth seekers, are best positioned to, in turn, train members how to purposefully minister to these new converts. This chapter provides young disciples with ideas that will motivate and teach members the ways to embrace converts into full activity.

Chapter Twelve: Concluding Thoughts—"Thou Shalt Speak"

The rights, authorities, and gifts of discipleship permit today's missionaries to do marvelous things in the name of Jesus Christ. As they prepare to receive this holy calling, young disciples should gain confidence that the powers of the priesthood are with them. Christ's Church and His chosen apostles bless, teach, and labor alongside "fellow missionaries" to gather Israel and bring the world His truth.

About the Authors

Robert Y. Cornilles

Robert Y. Cornilles is an international best-selling author and the Founder and CEO of Game Face, Incorporated, an executive training company serving more than 400 professional sports franchises, entertainment companies, universities, and corporations worldwide. A former full-time missionary and graduate of Brigham Young University, Brother Cornilles also serves as an adjunct professor at the BYU Marriott School of Business and a guest professor at Maryville University in St. Louis, Missouri.

As a volunteer, Brother Cornilles has served on several nonprofit boards, including Special Olympics of Oregon and the national advisory board of Positive Coaching Alliance based in Palo Alto, California. He was formerly the chairman of the board of the Cascade Pacific Council of the Boy Scouts of America. His various Church callings have provided him many opportunities to work with missionaries, youth and adults. Brother Cornilles and his wife Allison are the parents of three returned missionaries.

Taylor Halverson

Taylor Halverson is an aspiring master learner and an Entrepreneurship Professor in the BYU Marriott School of Business. He has discovered his life purpose to help people find and act on the best ideas and tools in order to experience enduring joy.

As an executive coach and entrepreneur, Taylor builds leaders and businesses while creating transformative professional and personal development experiences.

Taylor leads acclaimed travel tours to incredible locations throughout the world (Israel, China, India, Europe, Central America, and America's National Parks). Tour members have loved his irresistible enthusiasm, encyclopedic knowledge, spirit of adventure, and sense of fun.

Taylor is a prolific author and editor of twenty books and more than three hundred articles and a developer of breakthrough scripture study resources with Book of Mormon Central (ScripturePlus app & Come, Follow Me Insights videos with Tyler Griffin) and BYU's Virtual Scripture Group (3D Ancient Jerusalem project).

Taylor lives in Springville, Utah, with his wife Lisa and their two kids. He loves to spend time with his family on all sorts of adventures including exploring the nooks and crannies of the American West and Southwest, participating with geology and archaeology teams on location, creating and mixing electronic music, watching and discussing edifying shows, reading good books, playing games, learning, and laughing.

Taylor's academic training includes

BA, Ancient Near Eastern Studies, Brigham Young University
MA, Biblical Studies, Yale University
MS, Instructional Systems Technology, Indiana University
PhD, Instructional Systems Technology, Indiana University
PhD, Judaism & Christianity in Antiquity, Indiana University

Would you like a free humorous ebook from Taylor? Follow this link to request *Memoirs of the Ward Rumor Control Coordinator:* shorturl.at/koqO5

Learn more at taylorhalverson.com

www.ingramcontent.com/pod-product-compliance
Lightning Source LLC
Chambersburg PA
CBHW021225090426
42740CB00006B/388